Controversies in Sociology
edited by
Professor T. B. Bottomore and
Professor M. J. Mulkay

21
Citizenship and Capitalism

Controversies in Sociology

1. SOCIAL THEORY AND POLITICAL PRACTICE
   Brian Fay
3. SOCIALISM: THE ACTIVE UTOPIA
   Zygmunt Bauman
6. THE LIBERATION OF WOMEN
   A Study of Patriarchy and Capitalism
   Roberta Hamilton
7. MARX AND THE END OF ORIENTALISM
   Bryan S. Turner
8. SCIENCE AND THE SOCIOLOGY OF KNOWLEDGE
   Michael Mulkay
9. INTELLECTUALS AND POLITICS
   Robert J. Brym
10. SOCIOLOGY AND HISTORY
    Peter Burke
11. A THIRD WORLD PROLETARIAT?
    Peter Lloyd
12. MAX WEBER AND KARL MARX
    Karl Löwith
    Edited and with an Introduction by
    Tom Bottomore and William Outhwaite
13. POSITIVISM AND SOCIOLOGY: EXPLAINING SOCIAL LIFE
    Peter Halfpenny
14. AESTHETICS AND THE SOCIOLOGY OF ART
    Janet Wolff
15. CAPITAL, LABOUR AND THE MIDDLE CLASSES
    Nicholas Abercrombie and John Urry
16. THE LIMITS OF RATIONALITY
    An Essay on the Social and Moral Thought of Max Weber
    Rogers Brubaker
17. THEORIES OF MODERN CAPITALISM
    Tom Bottomore
18. THE KNOWLEDGE ELITE AND THE FAILURE OF PROPHECY
    Eva Etzioni-Halevy
19. A RECONSTRUCTION OF HISTORICAL MATERIALISM
    Jorge Larrain
20. CITIES, CAPITALISM AND CIVILIZATION
    R. J. Holton

Citizenship and Capitalism

The Debate Over Reformism

BRYAN S. TURNER
The Flinders University of South Australia

London
ALLEN & UNWIN
Boston   Sydney

© Bryan S. Turner, 1986
This book is copyright under the Berne Convention
No reproduction without permission. All rights reserved

**Allen & Unwin (Publishers) Ltd,
40 Museum Street, London WC1A 1LU, UK**

Allen & Unwin (Publishers) Ltd,
Park Lane, Hemel Hempstead, Herts HP2 4TE, UK

Allen & Unwin, Inc.,
8 Winchester Place, Winchester, Mass. 01890, USA

Allen & Unwin (Australia) Ltd,
8 Napier Street, North Sydney, NSW 2060, Australia

First published in 1986

British Library Cataloguing in Publication Data

Turner, Bryan S.
   Citizenship and capitalism: the debate over
   reformism. – (Controversies in sociology; v. 21)
   1. Civics   2. Capitalism
   I. Title   II. Series
   323.6'5   JA88.U66
ISBN 0–04–301241–8
ISBN 0–04–301242–6 Pbk

Library of Congress Cataloging in Publication Data

Turner, Bryan S.
   Citizenship and capitalism.
   (Controversies in sociology; 21)
Bibliography: p.
Includes index
1. Citizenship.   2. Politics, Practical.
3. Capitalism.   4. Labor and laboring classes.
5. Minorities.   I. Title.   II. Series.
JF801.T87 1986   323.42'3   85–22813
ISBN 0–04–301241–8 (alk. paper)
ISBN 0–04–301242–6 (pbk.: alk. paper)

Set in 10 on 12 point Times by Phoenix Photosetting, Chatham
and printed in Great Britain by Biddles Ltd., Guildford, Surrey

Aux armes, citoyens
Rouget de Lisle (1760–1836)

Contents

		page	xi
Preface			xi
Introduction: What is the Controversy?			1
1	The Origins of Citizenship		13
2	Politics and Reformism		27
3	Social Struggles		53
4	Social Movements		85
5	Individualism and Citizenship		106
6	Conclusion		134
References			143
Index			157

Preface

This study of the dynamic relationship between politics and economics in late capitalist societies forms part of a larger series of studies on ideology which started with *The Dominant Ideology Thesis* (Abercrombie, Hill and Turner, 1980). In these studies of ideology, various aspects of politics, religion, law and economic doctrine have been analysed in terms of the requirements of the capitalist mode of production. The general theme of these studies is that the importance of ideology has been frequently exaggerated in contemporary Marxist sociology, that the working classes are not incorporated by an overarching dominant ideology and that – where ideology has any effect – it is typically in organizing the coherence of a dominant class. In general, these inquiries suggest that late capitalism is quite peculiar in its structural requirements and represents a significant departure from the characteristics which define competitive capitalism. If these conclusions are valid, then it raises a problem about the explanation of the coherence of modern capitalism, especially in periods of severe economic recession and social crisis.

In our earlier study of dominant ideologies in capitalism we emphasized the importance of what Marx had called the dull compulsion of economic relationships. We saw the ultimate coherence of any society in terms of the forces which are brought to bear on individuals, compelling them to accumulate or work or save; that is, we located the fundamental requirements of society in the production and reproduction of economic circumstances. Ideology may contribute to and aid such basic economic conditions but the role of ideology is characteristically contingent rather than determinant. It could be argued that such an explanation neglects the role of political factors in the organization of capitalism and it has been argued in contemporary political sociology that the political process should be seen as relatively autonomous from economic requirements. The present study is an attempt to discuss this issue by considering the contribution of T. H. Marshall to the debate over the nature of modern capitalism through an examination of the growth of citizenship from civil to social rights.

I take the position that an extension of social rights is the outcome of political struggle and social movements whereby the working classes gained significant participation in capitalist society with the effect of influencing and limiting the profitability of capitalism. Thus there is something of a contradiction between class and citizenship. However, citizenship is not simply about class relationships since modern social movements have addressed the problems of women's rights, environmentalism, the status of children and ethnicity. Citizenship can be conceived as a series of expanding circles which are pushed forward by the momentum of conflict and struggle. This is not an evolutionary view of citizenship since these rights can also be undermined by economic recession, by right-wing political violence, by inflation and by the redefinition of social participation through the law. Citizenship expands under conditions of class conflict, popular struggle, warfare and migration.

This study has been significantly influenced by my own experience of migration and by my own attempt to come to terms with a multicultural society. This experience has been enriching, at least partly, as an outcome of an intellectually satisfying environment at the University at Flinders. In particular, I would like to thank Bob Holton, Allan Patience and Karen Lane for their lively interest in questions of social change, modernity and social rights under conditions of multiculturalism. In particular Karen Lane's thesis on the state's interest in unity (with special reference to class and citizenship in broadcasting arrangements in Australia) provided a significant contribution to this debate. In this respect, this present study can be seen as part of the critique of the nostalgic assumptions of traditional society, traditional sociology and at least in part an affirmation of the potentially progressive dimensions of modern democracy despite ongoing inequality and repression.

Ina Cooper and Susan Manser laboured artfully to transform my ideas into a text. If one can talk about the ownership of ideas, I alone claim responsibility for the views expressed here.

BRYAN S. TURNER

Introduction

What is the controversy?

THE PROBLEM OF SOCIAL ORDER

One central theoretical issue in classical sociology was concerned with the explanation of the bases of social order and stability. It can be argued that sociology was itself a response to the crises of European society which followed in the wake of the French Revolution and the Industrial Revolution (Nisbet, 1967). Thus, in the sociology of Emile Durkheim, social order was explained as the outcome of new patterns of reciprocity emerging from the social position of labour and a new set of general social values associated with either socialism or nationalism (Durkheim, 1962; Giddens, 1978). In twentieth-century sociology explanations of social coherence have rested typically on the work of Talcott Parsons who – in *The Social System* (1951) – located the roots of social stability in the existence of a system of common values and common patterns of socialization and internalization. Social systems were integrated where their members were motivated by common norms in search of common goals as specified by a system of overarching values (Parsons, 1951, 1966, 1971). In this tradition of sociological inquiry, industrial societies survive despite much internal conflict and deviance, because there is a system of general values, a set of institutions linking the individual to society and a variety of processes and patterns which contain the destructive forces of the market place.

Against this tradition it has been asserted that human societies are in fact characterized by a good deal more conflict, violence and contradiction than Parsons' functionalism would suggest. Societies cannot be said to be coherent or stable since manifestly they are divided into conflicting and competing social classes and social groups (Bottomore, 1975; Rex, 1981). Parsons' theories were also held to be tautological since the only evidence for the function of an institution is precisely the survival of that institution. Furthermore, it was suggested by a variety of commentators that Parsons' sociology could neither explain social change nor deal adequately with questions of power and dominance (Dahrendorf, 1968). It became common therefore in sociology in the 1960s to draw a sharp distinction between the functionalism of Parsonian sociology with its emphasis on value consensus and Marxist sociology with its concentration on conflict and change (Cohen, 1968). In contemporary sociology this division is no longer so sharply drawn or so confidently asserted. For example, it is arguable that the analytic assumptions of Marxism and Parsonian sociology are often parallel rather than opposed. Parsons himself argued that any explanation of social stability would necessarily be an explanation of social change (Parsons, 1961). Although there are important political, theoretical and evaluative differences between the Parsonian and Marxist traditions, it is difficult to distinguish Marxist from Parsonian structuralism in terms of its underlying analytical logic (Turner, 1981; Alexander, 1982). One illustration of this parallel would be the importance of the concept of ideology in modern Marxism in relationship to the centrality of the idea of common culture in Parsons' sociology (Abercrombie, Hill and Turner, 1980). In order to explain the absence of a revolutionary tradition in the working class in contemporary capitalist societies, Marxists have often adopted the concept of hegemony from Antonio Gramsci. It is the dominant ideology which has the effect of incorporating the working classes by instilling notions of the legitimacy and fairness of modern property relationships. This dominant ideology is an all-pervasive hegemonic culture in the advanced capitalist societies which is disseminated by the mass media, the school system, the churches and the reformist trade unions (Connell, 1977). It is difficult to see how in analytic terms this view of ideology as an all-embracing hegemonic culture which legitimates the social structure and motivates individuals via normative commitments to the political system can be differentiated from the functionalist view of the value system as an all-embracing system of values which is internalized through the family, the school and the local community (Lechner, 1984). In the absence of a revolutionary tradition and in the absence of a major crisis in the core capitalist states, Marxists have often turned their attention to the analysis of social stability (despite the business cycle) and their explanation of the coherence of capitalism has been frequently based upon the notion of a dominant ideology rather than upon an analysis of economic processes and conditions.

WHAT MARX REALLY SAID

This exaggerated emphasis on the importance of the superstructure in some versions of modern Marxism is a departure from the economic analysis of capitalism which Marx offered in his mature writing, especially in *Capital* (1924, Vol. I). Marx's account of capitalism is clearly complex if not contradictory and interpretations of it are legion. There is no such thing as an authoritative interpretation of Marx but it seems evident that he placed considerable emphasis on the economic structure of capitalism in order to explain its character and likely development. In England, the origins of capitalism had required the primitive accumulation of wealth through the enclosures of peasants' lands; this expropriation created a supply of wool which came to generate the conditions for the textile industry. The worker is now forced to comply with the structure of capitalist relationships because he is no longer self-sufficient; he is no longer able to support himself on his own plot of land; he is forced to comply with the demand of capital for labour in an open market-place where, to quote one of Marx's favourite expressions, he is 'free to sell his labour'. He is compelled to obey because he has a choice between starvation and employment, and this is what Marx meant by the dull compulsion of economic relationships in capitalism. In a similar fashion the capitalist is compelled to make profit in order to survive the competitive forces of the capitalist market-place. The logic of capitalist relationships compels the worker to work and forces the capitalist to make a profit regardless of their beliefs, motives and intentions. The revolutionary nature of capitalism resided in the fact that it was not sentimental towards traditional patterns and was indifferent to the particularistic character of labour, money and wealth.

Of course Marx felt that if this dull compulsion could be

legitimized itself by ideology, political doctrine or religion then this was certainly to the advantage of the owner of capital. If the worker could be induced to believe that the system was natural or divinely sanctioned or inherently moral, then no doubt capitalism would be supported by such doctrine. Thus, in *The German Ideology*, Marx and Engels suggested that capitalism was supported by the ruling ideas of the ruling class and when Marx wrote about fetishism in *Capital* he suggested that these economic relationships commonly assumed a mystified form in the belief systems of the participants within capitalism. However, his basic argument is economic and this economic argument says that capitalism depends upon the compulsion of the worker to submit to the logic of the market place and what he called the despotic order of the factory. These economic forces clearly had the support of the state, the law and the ideological system of capitalism but the lynch pin in the system was the economic relationship between capital and labour in the market place. It is on the basis of this argument that Louis Althusser argued that in capitalism it is the economic structure which is both determinant and dominant; by contrast the peasant was not entirely subordinated by economic relationships in feudalism and hence there was a need for political and ideological subordination (Althusser and Balibar, 1970).

THE COHERENCE OF CONTEMPORARY CAPITALISM

In present-day capitalist society few people starve (to death) as a consequence of unemployment or the withdrawal of their labour. Of course many people live in abject poverty and some die as a consequence of a combination of circumstances, typically including senility, illness, poor housing, unemployment and poverty. What then compels or induces the worker to work? Despite the appalling record of occupational illness and accident in capitalism and despite the exploitative nature of hierarchically organized factory production, the advantages of work over unemployment are relatively obvious: access to scarce resources in terms of health, education and housing; the advantages of credit-worthiness; access to consumption goods through hire-purchase arrangements; and finally self-esteem within the community. In negative terms the element of compulsion is located in the stigma of poverty and the labelling of the dependent unemployed on welfare and charity (Waxman, 1977; Spicker, 1984). Politicians committed to monetarism would clearly like to make unemployment more painful than it is under welfare policies in order to strengthen the commitment to employment even at relatively low wages. However, in both North America and Britain, monetarist policies have been difficult to pursue with anything like a pure economic logic. The economic decline of Great Britain in the postwar period, the decline of British manufacturing industries, the economic recession of the 1970s and the severe decline of the value of sterling in the 1980s have not brought about a situation where unemployment leads ultimately to starvation. It is clear, however, that there has been a sharp increase in the proportion of the population which is categorized as living on the margins of poverty.

Why does modern capitalism depart from the economic model of capitalism which we find in Marx's economic sociology? Part of the answer is to be found in the extension of social citizenship over the last hundred years as a consequence of working-class struggles, trade-union organizations and the effects of social democracy. In other words the full force of the market place is not felt by the working classes because the institutions of social welfare to some extent regulate the market and compensate for income inequality, poverty and unemployment. The vision of economic man as an individual in a competitive relationship which is at the heart of classical economics may be useful in the formulation of economic models but it is not appropriate as an empirical description of economic relationships in late capitalism. The individual capitalist is restrained by state intervention which regulates the money market, investment, inheritance and the running of the financial system. The worker is protected, however imperfectly, from the full rigour of the market as a consequence of the shield provided by the growth of unionism and the welfare system.

The importance of citizenship in relationship to both class and capitalism was at the core of T. H. Marshall's massive contribution to the sociology of welfare capitalism (Marshall, 1977, 1981). Marshall saw modern capitalism as a contradictory system in which the political process and the economic process were to some extent disjoined. The political sphere is relatively democratic and enables the working classes, minorities and marginal groups to achieve a certain degree of civil, political and social rights. Citizenship is an abatement of the class structure of capitalist economic relationships. The economy tends to generate inequalities in income and wealth whereas the political system is based upon the egalitarian principle of citizenship. In this respect political democracy and the class structure of capitalism stand in a contradictory relationship. An expansion of citizenship rights interferes with the market principle of capitalism, whereas an increase in the naked function of the market interferes with the enjoyment of egalitarian social rights.

THE CRITIQUE OF REFORMISM

T. H. Marshall's work has been widely influential in sociological studies of the contradictory relationship between parliamentary democracy and the free market of capitalism (Goldthorpe, 1978; Rose et al., 1984). His conception of the contradictory structure of capitalism is also to some extent implicit in the work of Bob Jessop whose analysis of the political shell of capitalism is especially important in understanding the relationship between parliamentary democracy, corporatism and modern politics (Jessop, 1972; 1974, 1982). Of course Marshall has also been more critically evaluated especially by those who see his sociology as a defence of reformism within a capitalist society, and his historical analysis of the expansion of citizenship rights has been criticized as an evolutionary view of development which fails to grasp the contradictory feature of the double-edged significance of citizenship. Citizenship rights do serve to extend human freedoms but they also continue to be points of social conflict. It may also be the case that Marx's critique of 'bourgeois freedoms' remains an important counter-argument to Marshall's liberal conceptualization of social relationships (Giddens, 1982). The principal objection to Marshall would thus be that, despite changes in the legal and political structure of capitalism, the basic inequality of the relationship between capital and labour has not been changed or significantly challenged. The possibilities for social mobility and social equality in capitalism remain essentially limited by the overriding need for profit and capital accumulation. Parliamentary democracy merely obscures rather than transforms the basic relationship between capital and labour (Maravall, 1979). Following Marx, one critique of capitalism would be that the alleged freedoms of speech, association and welfare are merely a sham. The alternative view is that social rights represent a genuine advancement of the working classes and a significant inroad into the free operation of the market. In capitalism therefore 'Citizenship hinders the carrying through of market principles; for example, a citizen has a right to health care regardless of any ability to pay' (Rose *et al.*, 1984, p. 152). From this perspective, working-class politics which aims to extend social rights in capitalism is a perfectly appropriate and radical activity. However, if citizenship is regarded as mere reformism, then working-class politics which pursues the aim of extending citizenship is also simply reformism which has the consequence of incorporating the working classes and stabilizing capitalism as an exploitative system.

REVISIONISM

When Marxists and critical theorists dismiss the growth of social citizenship as mere reformism, their model of history inevitably refers back to the problem of Marxist revisionism in the period since the 1890s when it first emerged in the German Social Democratic Party through the theories of Eduard Bernstein (Kolakowski, 1978, Vol. II). Bernstein rejected the idea that Marxism could be equivalent to a natural science based upon social laws of development; he also argued against the inevitability of capitalist crises based upon class polarization and he also rejected the idea that there had to be a violent socialist revolution to bring about the collapse of capitalism. Against a background where the German working classes had enjoyed increasing real wages, improvements in their social welfare and the achievement of a shorter working day, Bernstein argued that socialism in Germany could follow a British path achieving substantial socialist gains through the ballot box and conventional democratic politics. He assumed that the revolutionary conception of a radical transition to socialism was utopian terrorism and unrelated to the real conditions which existed in the industrial capitalist societies of Europe. Socialism could be achieved by evolutionary development without a necessary revolutionary break from one mode of production to another. In his analysis of German society he argued that the classes had not been polarized but there had been the emergence of a middle class and a white-collar class of technicians and administrators. He also thought that the development of the joint-stock system meant that wealth was not necessarily concentrated into a property-owning dominant class but was more widely spread through society. In general, Bernstein thought that changes in the nature of foreign markets had enabled capitalism to make pragmatic adjustments to economic crises and that capitalism had demonstrated its flexibility and capacity to cope with business cycles and crises of production and under-consumption. In his political perspective Bernstein saw that democracy was not simply a means to attain a social end but rather a value in its own right which was constitutive of socialism per se. Although Bernstein became the object of bitter criticism within the radical socialist movement, his view of social democracy was adopted in practice and implicitly by a number of European labour movements (Gay, 1952). More recently, some European Communist parties have adopted a new outlook which has come to be known as Euro-communism. This movement is part of a decentralization and de-Stalinization of socialism, but it was also a response to changing social and economic circumstances, especially with the emergence of the so-called new middle strata and the restructuring of the working classes.

The problem that lies behind these movements is the long-term relevance of orthodox Marxism to the analysis of the social structure of contemporary capitalism. A number of changes have occurred which have rendered Marx's account of capitalism increasingly problematic. While these changes are of course the subject of major debate, their features would include the following. First, there has been a relative decline in the proportion of the working classes in the total employment structure of contemporary capitalist societies (Abercrombie and Urry, 1983). New forms of technology and industrial production have reduced the number of workers in heavy industry in relationship to white collar and other sectors and to some extent this is related to the electoral decline of traditional socialist parties in a number of capitalist societies (Gorz, 1982). Secondly, there has been a depersonalization of property with the growth of joint-stock companies, the investment role of pension funds, the involvement of insurance companies in productive investments, and the involvement of the state in the reorganization of investment funding (Scott, 1979). Thirdly, the state plays an increasingly important part in stabilizing the crisis of capitalism, providing investment funds for future development, organizing the means for research and development, and providing some discipline of the working classes through the centralized negotiation of wages (Quinney, 1979). Fourthly, there has been a constant internationalization of the world-capitalist economy through the development of multinational corporations and as a consequence individual capitalist states have little scope for manoeuvre in organizing their internal economies against world economic trends. The capitalist state finds itself caught in these contradictory pressures between domestic needs and international economic structures (Radice, 1975). Fifthly, although the working classes have experienced a decline of real wages and standards of living in the 1980s as a consequence of economic recession, there is a paradoxical movement towards increased consumption through the development of new sales, financing and distributional systems in the advanced societies. The economic crisis is less pronounced at a subjective level than one would expect, because credit arrangements permit a continuity of consumption even in a context of rapid economic decline. One important feature of this is the growth of home ownership which in Great Britain increased from approximately 30 per cent of homes in 1950 to almost 60 per cent of homes in 1981. In Australia 69 per cent of all dwellings were classified as home ownership forms of tenure, which compared with 35 per cent in Sweden and 50 per cent in Britain. The consequences of home ownership are controversial (Kemeny, 1983). However, home ownership for the middle classes represents an important protection against inflation and subjectively in the working classes represents an experience of important social advancement (Rose et al., 1984).

Finally, these changes have had an important consequence for the nature of ideology and political loyalties in capitalist societies. The relationship between ideological legitimacy and the continuity of stable capitalist systems is weak and indirect since capitalism does not appear to require systematic ideological underpinning. That is, capitalism can 'tolerate' a high degree of personal and public deviance, and indeed to some extent promotes deviance. Even violence can be sold as a commodity. Since in principle the market is 'free' the government is held less responsible for economic outcomes than is the case in socialist societies where the economy is 'planned'. Whether or not democracy is a sham is the topic of this study, but in the area of consumption the citizens of western democracies have in the postwar period, despite economic downturns, experienced a considerable advance in their living standards over previous generations. Although the stability of capitalist societies is severely threatened by inflation and unemployment, changes in the provision of consumption have reduced the direct consequences of these changes. Even in a period of recession the idea that starvation is the consequence of unemployment is clearly no longer significantly applicable and its irrelevance is at least in part connected with the expansion of welfare rights and unionization.

THE CONTROVERSY

The liberal argument is that under capitalist conditions which permit various individual freedoms including freedoms of exchange, there is considerable scope for social and personal advancement; in particular capitalism, despite the business cycle, has both improved the standard of living of the majority of the populations of industrial societies and extended their political freedoms, at least by comparison with socialist and planned societies. The limited success of socialist and communist parties in western democracies is held to be evidence of the success of capitalism. The socialist critique of this liberal position involves a number of arguments. It is suggested that the doctrine of equality and freedom in capitalism is a mere sham, since massive inequality continues in capitalist society where large sections of the population live in poverty. There is thus a flat contradiction between promise and practice. It is also suggested by the socialist critique that capitalism leads to the enslavement of subordinate populations on its periphery as a consequence of colonialism and neocolonialism. What prosperity there is for the majority of workers in capitalist society is partly a consequence of the exploitation of colonial peripheries. It is also argued that, while there is democratic freedom in terms of the franchise, the ballot and equal voting rights, the political system is in fact dominated by the ruling class who own the effective means of wealth production. For some socialist critics, the failure of radical parties to gain significant electoral support is a consequence of the dominant ideology of capitalism, where the means of communication are owned by powerful elites who represent the property-owning class. Finally, it is suggested that the inequalities of capitalism can only be finally resolved by a revolutionary transition to a socialist society.

In this study, although I accept the socialist critique of the liberal position as a powerful alternative, I suggest that the underlying assumptions of this socialist critique are no longer relevant, or are incoherent or morally unacceptable. However, I also wish to transform the liberal view of capitalism as itself outdated and in need of serious revision, especially in the light of the social development of white colonial settler societies on the periphery of capitalism. Citizenship is not simply about class and capitalism but also involves debates about the social rights of women, children, the elderly and even animals. The traditional debate is thus too narrow and requires elaboration and expansion.

We need to see the political process as relatively autonomous and there are good grounds for supporting the revisionist position of Eduard Bernstein that democracy is a goal worth pursuing and not simply a means to achieve other ends. I argue that citizenship is a consequence of real and popular struggles against various forms of hierarchy, patriarchy, class exploitation and political oppression; the achievements of these struggles should not be dismissed as mere mystifications of capitalism or illusory forms of democracy. The political achievement of full citizenship where it involves significant social rights is a direct challenge to capitalism, but it is also a challenge to authoritarian forms of political rule. Although the notion of progress is now often regarded as utopian or evolutionary, there is an important principle of emancipation in the struggle for social membership and participation which citizenship confers (Wertheim, 1974). Citizenship is not simply about the abatement of class struggle in capitalism; it provides a major criterion for what it is to be a modern society based upon some notion of universalism and justice in opposition to local, particular and hierarchical attitudes and institutions. The societies of western industrial capitalism are essentially contradictory and there is an ongoing dynamic relationship between citizenship and the inequalities of the market place. The dynamic feature of capitalism is precisely the contradiction between politics and economics as fought out in the sphere of social citizenship.

1
The Origins of Citizenship

THE GREEK POLIS

Wherever there are political institutions and social groups with defined boundaries, there will be questions about the nature of citizenship, where citizenship means social participation. The very existence of a social boundary produces dilemmas with respect to defining insiders and outsiders. The rituals of inclusion and exclusion ultimately crystallize into criteria of political identity and participation. If we define citizenship therefore as an issue relating to social membership and participation then the question of citizenship is as old as human society as such. However, this definition is too vague and it is more meaningful sociologically to open our discussion of citizenship with Greek politics where the notion of the city-state and cultural membership became clearly identified in an articulate political philosophy – that is, in the works of Plato and Aristotle. In Greek politics there developed a distinctive appreciation of the benefits of political participation and the corresponding duties of the citizen in public life. According to some commentators, the Greek city-state resembled a modern private corporation in which the citizens were stock-holders. The members drew benefits from this corporation in time of need and thus the state provided for the orphan, the sick and the unprotected dependants of society. In return for this protection the able-bodied citizens were expected to provide services and render public duties (Gouldner, 1967).

In *The Republic*, Plato – in search of a definition of justice – outlines a paternalistic and totalitarian view of the state in which democracy is rejected partly because it provides no restraint on desire and subordinates the intellect to the rule of the many

(MacIntyre, 1967a). For Plato the problem of absolute political power was to be solved by the development of an altruistic ruling class which had been appropriately disciplined by philosophy and a cultured existence. This ruling class would be the antidote to the unreason of the majority, but would not exploit their absolute control over society in ways which were selfish and narrow. Plato identified the *polis* with *paideia* – that is, with the moral cultivation and education of its members – and this carried with it the implication that any unwarranted extension of the *polis* would lead to the diminution of culture and virtue.

Although the conception of Greek democracy is often held up in subsequent political theory as the ideal of participation in political life, the classical world was a world divided into either distinctive classes (Ste Croix, 1981) or into distinctive strata defined by authoritarian dominance (Runciman, 1983). Aristotle was aware that in certain city-states the workers (*banausoi*) had the benefits of full citizenship but he argued that such an inclusion of the workers was inappropriate. The main criterion of citizenship was the capacity to govern and to be governed, as a consequence of self-discipline and education, based upon full ownership of property. The true citizen is a person who knows how to obey and also how to command and on these grounds Aristotle excluded certain categories of persons from full political participation. For example, Aristotle argued that slaves and freed slaves were inappropriate as citizens. Similarly, women and children were only citizens in a very limited and qualified sense, and he went on to suggest therefore that the best form of government will not include workers under the category of citizen. Aristotle defined the citizen in the full sense as 'one who has a share in the privileges of rule' (Aristotle, 1962, p. 112). In the last analysis it is the ownership of property which confers full citizenship since it is property which meant that the citizen did not require manual labour to survive; the propertied citizen could thus devote himself to public service without the distraction of labour.

The problem of Greek public life was the conflict between the values and institutions of private achievement and competition versus the public requirements of altruistic service and co-operation. Greek citizens competed with each other in economic, political and cultural terms, and this very competitiveness periodically threatened the institution of public order. It was Nietzsche who noted that the competitiveness of Greek society took place on the sports field and in the public assemblies where free men competed physically and intellectually. For Nietzsche the excellence of Greek public life was that it provided a public space within which men could compete in intellectual argument, just as they fought each other physically in the game; it was this contest which provided a healthy means by which the will to power could find an outlet in a public and viable culture without threatening the social structure. Competition thus institutionalized the will to power in a society which encouraged heroic virtues (Strong, 1975). The struggle within and between the city-states constantly threatened the citizen with the prospect of their own slavery under the dominance of foreign powers. Original Greek democracy was also undermined by the growth of royal, magisterial control over the popular assemblies of the citizens, the attachment to magistracies of expensive civil duties and the slow destruction of the popular law courts which had been a crucial feature of classical athenian democracy (Ste Croix, 1981). The slow destruction of Greek democracy was completed by Roman dominance where the Roman ruling class sought to obliterate democratic institutions in favour of a more authoritarian form of control. The collapse of Greek democracy was in part the outcome of internal social processes and also a consequence of a failure of international relationships, which left the competing city-states exposed to the invasion of barbarians; Greek exclusiveness never resolved the contradictions between isolation, self-sufficiency and cultural development (Sabine, 1963). In the political culture which emerged in Roman times, through the influence of stoicism as embodied in the works of Seneca and Marcus Aurelius, there was a greater emphasis on the importance of the autonomous individual against the claims of public life. In Christian theology this relationship between the individual soul and the universality of the church gave rise to a redefinition of citizenship and political life, in a religious tradition where there was an essential conflict between politics in this world and the religious life in the next.

THE CITY OF GOD

Islam, Judaism and Christianity are typically defined as prophetic, monotheistic and literate religions. Despite these common features, the political shape of these faiths varied considerably according to their point of origin. The structural origins of a religion have a long-term and normative impact on later content both in doctrine and in practice (Turner, 1976). Thus Islam developed from the collapse of two existing empires and quickly assumed a military dominance within the middle east and North Africa as an imperial power. By contrast, Judaism was a confederacy of nomadic tribes bound together by a contractual obligation to Yahwe, but this confederacy was eventually dismembered by Roman imperial intervention (Turner, 1981). Christianity developed primarily as a religion of a subordinate class which set itself against this worldly politics but became eventually a state religion during the period of Charlemagne's rule (Wanlass, 1953). The Abrahamic religions are faiths based upon brotherly love but they are forced to come to terms with the politics of violence and they have done so under different conditions, partly depending on their relationship to political empires at their point of inception (Weber, 1965).

The Abrahamic faiths have made an important historical contribution to citizenship, despite their overt rejection of politics as a diversion from the true life of spirituality. The contribution of Christianity to the structure of modern societies has been clearly noted by Talcott Parsons in an article which has been unfortunately neglected in contemporary sociology (Parsons, 1963). The Abrahamic religions generally created a radical egalitarianism which specified a general criterion of group membership. Islam was the most fundamentally egalitarian of these faiths but Islamicate society emerged eventually as a military-slave system in which slave soldiers played an important role in the constitution of the Islamic community (Pipes, 1981). The importance of Christianity for the development of a political community was that it radically liquidated the particularistic bonds of blood in favour of a community grounded on faith as a universalistic element of social membership (Weber, 1958). The city in Christian culture developed as an association of free men bound together by doctrine and practice rather than linked together by blood and kinship. Although Judaism had equally radical elements of universalism, the God of the people became limited to a community defined by the particularistic criteria of Jewishness.

The second fundamental contribution of these religions to citizenship was the notion of a contract binding men to their God. This contractual relationship was most fully developed in the case of the Jewish Covenant but most forms of Christianity adopted this metaphor of the man–God relationship. This covenant was routinely celebrated in the rituals of sacrifice especially in the Christian eucharist. These religious notions that men are bound to their Gods through contracts provided the model by which human relationships could be conceptualized. Those who have bound themselves to God also find themselves bound to each other within a religious community. This democratic notion of choice in the formation of political units provided the basis for social contract theories of the state which came to prominence from the seventeenth century onwards. It can be claimed that Christianity provided through its political theology some of the fundamental conceptual points of subsequent political theory (Oestreich and Koenigsberger, 1982).

THE MODERNITY OF CITIZENSHIP

On the basis of these considerations, we can identify three elementary meanings of citizenship in Western societies. First, the citizen is merely the inhabitant of a city and in England we find references to the 'citiseins' in the early fourteenth century. For example, Wyclif refers in 1382 to 'a citeseyn or burgeys, of a citee not unknown'. A century later, Caxton refers to the 'cytezeyns of London'. Secondly, therefore, citizen simply means inhabitant or occupant and in this sense citizen is more or less equivalent to denizen. Finally, a citizen is a member of a state. Although ancient origins for the notion of the citizen as a member of a state or city-state can be found, I wish to argue that the concept of citizenship is essentially modern. Furthermore, the conditions which define modernity simultaneously define citizenship. The development of citizenship seems inextricably bound up with the development of modern social conditions.

The existence of the citizen presupposes a certain decline in the dominance of hierarchical social structures and the emergence of egalitarian horizontal relationships between persons defined in universalistic terms. The citizen thus presupposes the development of a secular environment where religion no longer dominates public debate and public identity. In association with this secularization process citizenship depends upon a growing freedom of exchange, belief and choice. Citizenship and its associated rights can be tied to the development of economic markets and expanding exchange relationships which have the consequence of undermining particularistic definitions of those persons involved in exchange (Goldmann, 1973; Smith, 1973; Simmel, 1978). Citizenship is also bound up with the growth of formal rational law which is indifferent to the ascriptive character of legal subjects. Formal law is one guarantee of equal judgement between citizens. We can reasonably argue that the processes that gave rise to modern societies necessarily gave rise to the modern notion of citizenship as an achieved status.

One important indicator of the development of modern citizenship would be the inclusion of women in the category of citizen. My argument is that while we can engage in debates about the ancient origins of citizenship, modern citizenship can be dated from the French Revolution and from the development of the idea of *citoyenne*, which appeared alongside *citoyen* during the revolution of 1789. The doctrines of the French Revolution, of course, have been criticized as empty and abstract (Habermas, 1974). In particular, references to the equality of *citoyennes* are now regarded as merely rhetorical postures (Silver, 1973). Burke found the claims of the French Revolution to be simply pretentious in his *Reflections on the Revolution in France* of 1790 (Macpherson, 1980); Immanuel Kant interrupted his afternoon walk in Königsberg on discovering that the revolution had brought about the fall of the Bastille; Hegel, despite his ambivalence with respect to the Revolution, remembered the fall of the Bastille by regularly offering a toast to its anniversary on 14 July. While the achievements of the French Revolution are often held to be less than the phraseology which the revolutionaries used, it is easy to dismiss the slogan 'Liberty, Equality and

Fraternity' partly because we now see the French Revolution through the eyes of the Terror, through the Napoleonic period and through the events of the restoration.

However, the Revolution remains critically important for a discussion of the development of citizenship for a number of reasons. First, it clearly linked the idea of citizenship rights with the debate about human equality (although the bourgeois leaders of the early waves of the Revolution had somewhat limited ideas about what would count as equality) and allied citizenship with the notion of community in the principle of social fraternity. The Declaration of the Rights of Man and of the Citizen thus set the conventional view of individual rights within a broad framework that pointed to the debate about universality as requiring both equality and community. Secondly, the French Revolution greatly developed the idea of national citizenship since the Declaration located sovereignty in the nation. The French Revolution contributed to an important institutional development of the state as a separate entity with specific subjects called citizens (Dyson, 1980). Thirdly, the Revolution joined citizenship to the quest for political liberation, and the transformation of the status of the Jews was an important element of this progressive dimension to the French revolutionary conflict. This new conception of national citizenship and liberation came to have a fundamental impact on the development of Zionism and movements of national liberation in the Middle East against Turkish-Ottoman control which transformed the political map of the region.

The sociological analysis of the French Revolution is highly controversial. Although the revolution has been seen conventionally as a struggle by the bourgeoisie against feudal dominance, the monarchy and the church, more recent interpretations have questioned this Marxist framework. Hobsbawm analysed the revolution as a bourgeois struggle for political control in which the Declaration embodied the classical principles of liberal radical thought (Hobsbawm, 1962). Similarly, George Rudé (1964) emphasized the importance of bourgeois interest in the formulation of the Declaration which owed a particular philosophical debt to Locke, Montesquieu and Rousseau. The French Revolution was seen by Barrington Moore (1966) as a social revolution which removed the principal obstacle to liberal democracy, although Moore did not place a special emphasis on the bourgeoisie. There are a number of problems, however, in these interpretations. Before the revolution the French industrial sector was very underdeveloped; there was relatively little development of adequate banking facilities; the social structure was largely dominated by small-scale agricultural production. The Revolution may, in fact, have inhibited and slowed down the process of industrialization. There was the loss of overseas markets, the official recognition of peasant landownership and British imperial supremacy was eventually confirmed by the aftermath of the Napoleonic wars. The first and most intensive wave of industrialization was achieved under the authoritarian empire of 1850–1860 (Fohlen, 1973). The outcome of the Revolution was paradoxical in that the continuity of rural society and the bureaucratization of rule reinforced the predominance of executive-administrative arrangements over parliamentary-representative arrangements, so that authoritarian rule predominated over civil rights (Skocpol, 1979, p. 178ff.).

Although the French Revolution had consequences which were incompatible with the liberal intentions of the French bourgeoisie or the radical intentions of the small working classes of Paris, the Revolution was a major feature of the rise of a modern concept of citizenship linked to social change, political liberation and economic equality. As Marx observed in his analysis of French politics, the revolutionary struggle had done much to undermine the accumulated rubbish of feudal conditions (Marx, 1973). It is relatively easy to over-emphasize the violence of the Terror by adopting a Whig view of history as the evolution of individual rights of liberty.

The violence and disruption of revolution stimulated the development of a social perspective on the individual as the product of collective forces. There is the argument that sociology itself is, at least in part, the product of the French Revolution (Nisbet, 1967) and there is clearly an important theme in French social thought linking Rousseau to Durkheim, which emphasized the moral authority of the group in relation to the individual. One feature of Rousseau's philosophy was the emergence of the citizen as the focal point of political philosophy and thus the 'fundamental moral category is not man but citizen' (Sabine, 1963, p. 581). It was Rousseau's own political citizenship in the city-state of Geneva which contributed to the idealized picture of political participation which he developed in his later writing. Whereas the English utilitarian tradition had emphasized the idea of the separate autonomous actor exercising his will in the public sphere, the French tradition of social theory which culminated in Durkheim regarded this egoistic individualism as immoral and placed a central emphasis on the notion of moral individualism. Durkheim associated egoistic individualism with the rising tide of suicides, social disruption and social pathology in late nineteenth-century France and stressed the importance of moral individualism which he associated with the philosophy of Kant and Rousseau. For Durkheim this moral individualism was compatible with the social requirements of a modern society and actually contributed to the stability of social relationships. In his sociology, therefore, individualism emerges as an institution rather than as the characteristic of economic man in a competitive struggle (Durkheim, 1969). In his political sociology, the role of the state is to provide some form of moral and social stability in a society constantly disrupted by economic advances and by the strains emerging between existing culture and rapid changes in the social division of labour. The isolated citizen within the market had to be linked to the state via a series of new professional and trade associations and it was this intermediary structure within civil society that Durkheim argued would be significant in overcoming the alienation of economic individualism (Giddens, 1978).

CITIZENS, CLASSES AND CAPITALISM

From this brief outline of some crucial features in the development of citizenship, it is possible to define as an ideal type a continuum between premodern civil citizenship and contemporary national citizenship. Premodern societies are hierarchically organized in such a way that inequality is taken to be a natural characteristic of human beings. Membership of the social collectivity is based largely upon blood and property so that social structure depends upon the stability of patriarchal authority. In premodern societies there is a close relationship between the patriarchal authority of the king, the dominance of the head of the household and the authority of religious institutions. The secular authority of king and father was modelled upon the sacral authority of divinity. Membership of the social group was thus often defined in religious terms and entry into the social group was via a system of collective rituals (Rites de Passage). Non-membership is constituted by alien outsiders who are ritually excluded from membership by various strategies which have the effect of reinforcing the sacred boundary of the society. When a state begins to emerge in this system, it is normally clothed in some form of religious language, so that in Judaism the Ark of the Covenant was the symbol of political membership. Although some primitive notion of citizenship evolves in this environment, the hierarchical organization of statuses, the authoritarian character of patriarchy and the limited notion of citizenship as a public identity prevent the emergence of a fully organized egalitarian notion of social and national citizenship. The mirror-image structure of citizenship in modern societies is organized around a dichotomous and alternative set of principles. Modern citizenship presupposes some notion of equality, an emphasis on universalistic criteria and a secular system of values to reinforce claims and obligations. Societies organized on this principle emphasize contract over status, the dominance of secular reality over the sacred, the importance of universalism over locality and particularity, and the importance of extending citizenship rights to women and children so as to call into question the dominance of patriarchy.

It will be obvious that this ideal typical continuum is a summary of classical sociology which sought to distinguish modern from premodern society in terms of a distinction between status and contract, community and association, religious and secular, and hierarchical and egalitarian structures (Nisbet, 1967). It will also be obvious that this interpretation of citizenship as a category in opposition to hierarchy and ascription follows closely the idea of the pattern variables in the sociology of Talcott Parsons (Parsons, 1951). The Parsonian scheme has been used as a category for the classification of processes of modernization in which social change is conceptualized in terms of a transition from ascription to achievement (Hoselitz and Moore, 1966).

Implicit in the argument of this chapter has been the assumption that the conditions which produce modern society (and in particular the capitalist version of modern society) also produce modern national–social citizenship. Capitalism undermines hierarchical, particularistic, patriarchal and religious institutions and values, while promoting a society based simply upon the cash nexus where there are no traditional or moral assumptions about social relationships. Through exchange relationships, capitalism promotes the growth of a universalistic culture and by emphasizing the autonomy of the consumer contributes to the emergence of individualism. In general terms, capitalism promotes contractual relationships rather than status hierarchies and the idea of social contract as the basis of government is perfectly compatible with capitalist economic relationships. Capitalism thus generates a set of institutions which favour the emergence of citizenship and indeed capitalism requires citizens as informed and as 'free' agents in the market place. As Marx recognized, capitalism is a revolutionary force which undermines the rubbish of agrarian and traditional society. The slogans adopted by the bourgeoisie in competitive capitalism (namely liberalism, the laissez-faire economy, the night-watchman state and the importance of civil liberties) provide the ideological basis for early struggles of the working classes against the existing order. The working classes attempt to manipulate and use existing parliamentary structures to their own advantage, albeit under very restricted and exploitative conditions. The progressive dimension of capitalism promotes the emergence of citizenship by liquidating traditional and authoritarian institutions in favour of the compulsive control of the market. Furthermore, capitalism requires mobile labour and it was the mobility of labour which also further undermined the dominance of the country, the Church and the old regime. Geographical mobility promotes psychological mobility and creates the conditions whereby personalities can be developed with a strong interest in consumption and self-development through purchasing power. The achievement motive provides one of the ideological and psychological incentives for changing traditional markets.

However, while capitalism provides the conditions which stimulate and develop primitive notions of citizenship, capitalism also generates massive inequalities of a predominantly economic character. It is difficult to define capitalism independently of defining social class. The central characteristic of early capitalism is the division of society into those who own the means of production but do not labour and those who labour but do not own the means of production. Alongside these inequalities in ownership there necessarily develops inequality of income, status and prestige in the market place and in the place of work. The class structure of the market is complemented by the hierarchical organization of the factory which Marx described as a despotic form of government. Capitalism produces classes and citizens, but citizenship is difficult to achieve in a society structured by social classes.

The working classes and other social groups combine together to resist and change class inequality through political action and resistance in economic and social terms. Where citizens are successful in achieving greater equality, control and democracy, they necessarily interfere with the working of profit and accumulation in the economic system. The political organization of classes to promote citizenship necessarily attacks one of the basic roots of capitalism, namely the inequality between property owners and workers. Thus the more capitalism develops in terms of the class principle, the more it works against the possibility of citizenship. The success of the working classes, popular movements and subordinate social groups to expand and defend citizenship impinges upon the class principle in capitalism. This view of capitalism and citizenship is derived directly from T. H. Marshall who developed it in lectures given in 1949 (see Marshall, 1977). The basic idea of these lectures was later elaborated under the notion of the 'hyphenated society' in *The Right to Welfare* (Marshall, 1981).

In his studies on citizenship and class, Marshall considered the development of citizenship from the eighteenth to the twentieth centuries in England and divided citizenship into three separate rights – namely, civil, political and social rights. He argued that in the eighteenth century there was a considerable development and expansion of civil rights which were primarily concerned with legal status and these civil rights were defended through the courts. In the nineteenth century there was a corresponding development of political rights (especially the franchise). In the twentieth century there was an expansion of social rights as a consequence of wartime conditions and working-class struggles for benefits in a welfare state. One example of a social right was the universal right to an elementary education. Marshall argued that while civil and political rights were based upon a notion of equality they did not seriously threaten or undermine the working of capitalism but at most represented a form of 'class abatement'. Indeed, to function effectively, capitalism required the development of civil and political rights since these also embraced the institutions of contract, fair exchange and economic individualism. However, the social rights of the twentieth century were the basis of a welfare system which was in contradiction with the class principle of capitalism, and twentieth-century citizenship and the class structure of capitalist society 'have been at war' (Marshall, 1977, p. 121). Marshall would agree with Marx's observation that the liberal or utilitarian view of rights was the expression of class interest and that the liberal view of civil rights was essentially individualistic. These individual rights were not only compatible with capitalism but also possibly required by the capitalist market structure; however, Marshall thought that the working-class struggle for participation and representation had given rise to a new form of social right, which was the basis of a welfare system, and these social rights embodied real as opposed to illusory principles of equality.

CONCLUSION

The expansion of citizenship is complex and has a number of causal elements. It can be argued that the universalistic element in the Abrahamic faiths laid the ideological foundation for a universalistic definition of social membership not based upon blood or kinship. The peculiar features of occidental cities may also be associated with the decline of extended kinship ties as the basic definition of political participation. There were also important developments in law which corresponded to the requirements of a rational system of litigation; the Roman legal system and the growth of natural law reduced the ad-hoc element in legal decision-making. Furthermore, the growth of exchange relationships, the expansion of markets and the development of a modern system of money made possible the growth of autonomous individuals and undermined the importance of local, religious or particularistic definitions of the social person. The point of this argument is to suggest that the conditions for the growth of modern society were also the conditions for the growth of citizenship.

The critical factor in the emergence of citizenship is violence – that is, the overt and conscious struggle of social groups to achieve social participation. The primary instance of this violence is class conflict and we can define the main issue in class relationships as an issue about genuine participation and control. While class and class structure are important determinants of citizenship we must also consider new social movements (especially feminism) as crucial to the development of welfare rights. These social movements have historically had their most significant impact under conditions of war, and warfare thus represent the second illustration of violence as the basis of citizenship. One further feature of the emergence of citizenship under conditions of conflict is the historical importance of migration, since it is migration which undermines rural, hierarchical and stable social relationships. Migration is itself frequently the outcome of various forms of violence, where the migrant seeks escape in a new social environment.

2
Politics and Reformism

MARX AND THE JEWISH QUESTION

The debate about the social rights of Jews and the social location of Judaism was a significant feature of social philosophy in the nineteenth century and contributed to the evolution of theories concerning the status of minority groups within the community. The Jews were thought to be in many respects anomalous in the context of an emerging urban and secular society. This anomaly was important in the development of a Marxist view of working-class politics, but it also had a significant role to play in the development of sociology. For example, the Dreyfus Affair was crucial to the development of Durkheim's view of political sociology and the political status of the Jews in France became a touchstone in the divisions between the republican left and the catholic right (Marrus, 1971). The debate about the nature of the Jewish community and the history of Jewish assimilation and anti-Semitism provide an important illustration of the more general features of civil rights during the nineteenth century. The relationship between Marxism and the Jewish question provides one important location for the debate about reformism in the context of a capitalist society where there is massive economic inequality. The so-called 'Jewish question' was important in the biography of the Marx family but, more importantly, was formative in the development of Marx's political analysis of capitalist society.

The defeat of Napoleon created the context in which the monarchies of Europe could re-establish the prerevolutionary conservative social structure, which meant the cancellation of a variety of civil liberties. Napoleon's legal code in proclaiming the importance of human equality had transformed the civil status of

Jews in France and Germany. In the period of conservative restoration, Frederick William III was particularly forceful in restoring the old regime in Prussia with the aid of the landowning aristocracy and undermined the aspirations of the German liberal bourgeoisie in the towns. With the promulgation of the anti-Jewish laws of 1816, Heinrich Marx found it difficult to continue with his legal practice while remaining a Jew but, since Heinrich Marx was a follower of deism and the Enlightenment, he found the transition from the synagogue to the church relatively easy and joined the church in 1817, a year before the birth of his eldest son Karl. As a liberal and rationalist, Heinrich Marx was committed to the idea of individual emancipation and to Jewish assimilation within the established order (Berlin, 1978). In his childhood Karl Marx was brought up in this liberal culture where he developed 'a very distant and colourless deistic conception of God' (McLellan, 1973, p. 11). During this period, the 'Jewish question' emerged in Prussia as one division between liberals who thought that Jewish citizens should be given equal rights, on the grounds that they would then abandon their peculiar customs, and the conservatives who were committed to the notion of a Christian state, opposing Jewish emancipation on the view that Jews could never be Prussianized. In August 1842 Marx began to interest himself in this issue through reading the anti-Semitic articles of the editor of the *Kolnische Zeitung* which was arguing for a form of apartheid for Jews in Germany. Marx's interest was further stimulated by the publication of Bruno Bauer's pamphlet on Jewish emancipation from the perspective of left Hegelianism. Bauer argued that complete political emancipation could only be achieved when both Christians and Jews abandoned the exclusive practices which divided the two religious communities. The exclusiveness of the Christian tradition was in fact inherited from Judaism which represented a static aspect of human history. The dynamics of history required the Jews to abandon their restrictive faith if political advancement was to be secured in Germany.

Marx used Bauer's argument as a convenient starting point for his own critique of the liberal view of politics. Marx's critique of Bauer's thesis was presented in two review essays in the *Deutsch-Franzosische Jahrbucher* in 1844 (Carlebach, 1978). Marx objected that Bauer's argument was too abstract and theological, since religious questions had to be dissolved into real social questions. The continuity of religious practice had little to do with the theological relationship between state and society, and little to do with purely political issues. The continuity of religion could only be understood in terms of the continuity of social relationships that produced the need for religion. It was only by transforming social conditions that the roots of religious belief could be attacked. Political emancipation could not be equated with human emancipation and thus Bauer had attacked the problem from the wrong end. Religious alienation was the outcome of a deeper social and human alienation which would be obliterated by the ultimate transformation of society as a whole. This was an important step in the development of Marx's central position that ultimately political issues have to be understood in their socioeconomic context. The political process is ultimately determined by the basic socioeconomic foundations of a society and thus the politics of Prussia were a function of the capitalist structure of the society. The ultimate solution to the Jewish question was the destruction of the divisions and alienation characteristic of capitalist society. Marx's objection to Bauer was thus part of his intellectual transition from Hegelianism to a materialistic view of history.

While Marx criticized the liberal solution to Jewish emancipation on the grounds that it was inadequate as a social analysis, Marx was also critical of Moses Hess's version of Zionism which he regarded as largely utopian. Although Hess was a valuable ally of Marx and Engels he was regarded by Marx as an idealistic enthusiast whose ideas were somewhat naive. Marx and Engels were not consistently sympathetic to the autonomy of small nations and saw nationalism as somewhat remote from the real issue of a proletarian revolution. Marx's opposition to liberal views of Judaism and to Zionism became the official position of the German Social Democratic party, and it was Kautsky who reaffirmed the notion that Zionism was romantic and reactionary. Thus, Marxism has conventionally argued that the civil rights of minorities can only be resolved in the last analysis by revolutionary politics and the total re-structuring of society. In Marxism the civil-rights issue tends to be regarded as a product of more fundamental class relationships. Racism and fascism are seen to be endemic to capitalism as a class system.

MARX AND DEMOCRACY

Because Marx was a sharp critic of bourgeois democracy, it is sometimes assumed that Marx was indifferent or opposed to democracy as such. A number of writers have sought to undermine this assumption by asserting that it is impossible to imagine a socialist policy which was not fundamentally democratic. It is occasionaly argued therefore that what Marx is really advocating is the full democratization of society at all levels and that his criticism is directed against superficial, formal and merely political structures of the democratic process. Marx was obviously aware that criticism of democracy often came from the extreme right and that it was important to distinguish Marxist from other criticisms of the democratic process. It was also clear to him that while bourgeois democracy was inadequate it represented a challenge to traditional aristocratic authoritarianism and that working-class politics very typically assumed a political – democratic dimension. Marx's view of politics and in particular of democracy thus turns out to be fairly complex (Draper, 1974).

Marx argued, with special reference to the American case, that capitalist societies were based upon 'a democratic swindle' (Marx, 1961, p. 271), because they abused the democratic institutions of the political system in order to stabilize the social dominance of the capitalist class. Marx's critique was not aimed so much at democracy but at the abuse of democracy by the dominant class to guarantee the continuity of its rule. Marx also thought, however, that the democratic forms of capitalist society could be appropriated and expanded by popular struggle from below and that the democratic swindle could be turned against the dominant social class in the interests of popular sovereignty. While Marx's negative view of bourgeois democracy is commonly emphasized in commentaries on his political sociology, it is clear that he also considered that, when appropriated by the working classes, the democratic forms of capitalist society could come to undermine the foundations of bourgeois society. Thus, in *Class Struggles in France*, Marx envisaged the possibility of socialism being achieved through the ballot box and parliamentary democracy, and this feature of his argument was reinforced by Engels' 1895 introduction to that work. The belief that the working classes could transform capitalism primarily through parliamentary politics was espoused by many later Marxists, among them Karl Kautsky, the Austro-Marxists and, more recently, the Eurocommunists.

These revisionist and reformist interpretations of socialist politics were severely criticized and rejected by Lenin and by Rosa Luxemburg. Lenin was concerned to resist the growing influence of both revisionism and economism which he associated in particular with Bernstein and Kautsky in the Russian context; Lenin wished to emphasize the importance of the political process and the significance of education in transforming the consciousness of the workers. He argued that in all countries the working classes were only able to develop a trade-union consciousness – that is, the notion that it is necessary to combine to fight employers and to force the government to pass appropriate legislation to protect the working classes from the full rigours of a capitalist market. In order to convert this trade-union consciousness into a revolutionary perspective, it was necessary for the party to play an educational role in the leadership of the working classes. While the workers sought to improve their conditions of work, it was the task of social democracy to abolish the conditions of wage-labour – that is, to undermine capitalism itself. This necessary conflict between the working classes and the capitalist system could be understood from the scientific perspective of Marxism, but it could not be grasped by the workers without the intervention of the party as a vanguard of the revolution. The party had to be centralized, disciplined, hierarchical and well organized in order to bring about this conversion of trade-union consciousness into genuine revolutionary beliefs.

Lenin's view of the party and of the relationship between the party and the consciousness of the working classes has been the subject of much controversy and interpretation. Rosa Luxemburg accused Lenin of Blanquism in which a small well-organized group would through a *coup d'état* bring about the sudden downfall of the capitalist regime in advance of working-class organizations. Blanquism is consequently regarded as a romantic and elitist view of revolutionary politics which treated the working classes as largely passive in the historical destruction of capitalism (Harding, 1977; Kolakowski, 1978, Vol. II). In evaluating Lenin's view of revolutionary politics it is important to locate his views on strategy in the social and political context of Russian society where a strong bourgeois liberal regime had not developed and where the working class was somewhat fragmented and immature. The need for a well organized party was fairly significant in this Russian context, but the conditions obtaining in Germany, Italy and Britain were clearly very different (Plamenatz, 1954).

The existence of welfare institutions and forms of political democracy in capitalism clearly present problems for Marxist theory and political practice. The dominant position in Marxism is to treat political democracy in capitalism as a sham which has the consequence of stabilizing and conserving bourgeois hegemony. Marx was thus quite scathing about the superficiality of bourgeois democracy which limited democratic activity to a merely political context. Against this dominant position, there is evidence that both Marx and Engels came to accept the possibility that the working class could achieve its revolutionary ends through the existing democratic structures of capitalism (Duncan, 1973). In addition Marx adhered to a view of democracy which was distinctively reminiscent of a position adopted by Rousseau in that Marx objected to the indirect nature of democracy in a capitalist society where bureaucratic forms and state power were prominent. Genuine democracy involved direct participation in the political process and thus Marx saw the state in capitalist society as repressive and incompatible with this radical conception of democratic activity (Lefebvre, 1968). It is difficult to reconcile Marx's view of direct democracy with Lenin's view of the party since Marx insisted upon the importance of *praxis* as constitutive of human agency. Thus in the theses on Feuerbach, Marx insisted that practical consciousness was an essential determinant of human character and rejected elitist assumptions in conventional materialism. In addition, Marx in the Preface to the *Critique of Political Economy* had argued that it was social being which determined consciousness. On the basis of that argument, we would assume that the consciousness of the working classes was determined by their class experiences and that trade unionism under trade-union consciousness would be a direct manifestation of the workers' struggle to gain control over the workplace. It is difficult to know how the consciousness of the party would be necessarily superior to that of organized labour, and it would be difficult to know how the ideology of the party could be democratically imposed over that of class. This possibility of a fundamental difference between the consciousness of the working classes and the consciousness of the party has given rise to a variety of solutions in theoretical Marxism but in general the validity of these solutions is less than persuasive or striking. The reconciliation of these gaps normally takes the form of a distinction between class-in-itself and class-for-itself, where the party plays an educational role in raising the consciousness of the workers to that of party members. This distinction has given rise to a variety of terminological contrasts such as contingent and necessary consciousness (Mészáros, 1971) between true and false consciousness, and between actual and imputed class consciousness (Lukács, 1971). Contemporary Marxism as a result has given much emphasis to Gramsci's concept of hegemony and to the importance of ideological critique, radical education and the development of alternative perspectives to those which are dominant in capitalism.

OBJECTIONS TO DEMOCRACY

We have seen that classical Marxism developed a profound criticism of democratic forms in capitalism which were seen as a 'swindle' because they mystified the real nature of capitalism which is exploitative and repressive. Criticisms of democracy in capitalism are clearly not the exclusive property of mainstream Marxism but are widespread in a variety of political traditions including that of liberalism itself. It is common to assume that, for a variety of social, bureaucratic and political reasons, democracy cannot function effectively and openly in a modern complex industrial society. These criticisms of democracy range from relatively trivial commentaries on the problem of sampling opinions to more fundamental analyses of the biased social composition of parliament and cabinet. These critical observations on democracy are bound up with a wider concern for the problem of the state in capitalist society.

Within a variety of sociological and Marxist traditions, it is thus commonplace to observe that capitalist society is controlled by some form of ruling class or power elite which in fact dominates society regardless of the presence of democratic institutions. Whereas pluralist political theory suggests that capitalism is, in terms of its political institutions, characterized by the open competition of a variety of power groups or elites, other theorists argue that there is a cohesive ruling class which allegedly acts in a relatively cynical, coherent and consistent fashion to buy off discontent through welfare institutions under the umbrella of democratic participation. For example, it has been suggested that the political institutions of capitalist society rely upon the 'sustained growth of the total cake for buying off the discontent of the less privileged, and the general softening of manners, and the reduction in the severity of social sanctions, is presumably connected with this continuous rivalry' (Gellner, 1979, p. 29). Similarly, another critic of the liberal tradition has suggested that the emergence of a welfare state was 'necessary to buy off politically dangerous discontent. However, the welfare and regulatory state has not altered the essential nature of the capitalist market society' (Macpherson, 1966, p. 57). The general theme of these criticisms is that democracy in capitalism is largely illusory and that the development of welfare is intentionally aimed at placating social discontent without any fundamental change in the system as a whole.

In this study I shall focus on one component of this critique of welfare capitalism – namely, that working-class activity to secure welfare rights has the unintended consequence of incorporating the working classes within the capitalist system. This function of welfare rights is reinforced by a ruling class which exists behind the shield of allegedly popular democratic forms and processes. Parliamentary politics acts as a safety valve for class conflict and syphons off discontent from a variety of underprivileged sectors of society. The dominant class is held together by common interests and experience and, while politics takes the form of a pluralistic competition between interest groups at the level of parliament, the real structure is the structure of class relationships which is the principal feature of civil society in the capitalist system. It is reformism which explains the continuity of capitalism, despite periodic economic crises and political disruptions. While there is much industrial conflict and competition in capitalism, this is typically handled through the institutionalization of conflict under the control of the state in the final interests of the capital class. Strikes and other forms of industrial disruption are merely forms of organized competition in which the working classes through their trade-union representatives seek to improve their position in capitalism rather than seeking to transform capitalism into a socialist system. It is reformism which thus explains the largely apolitical and conservative character of the working classes in western industrial capitalism.

A CRITIQUE OF THE CRITICISM OF REFORMISM

Incorporationism

In contemporary Marxist theory, the western working class is commonly seen as a defeated class inside the capitalist system. For example, Nicos Poulantzas (1973), while frequently referring to the popular struggle of the working classes, makes relatively little space in his theoretical system for the effectivity of class struggle against the system of control in capitalist society and his theory of class structure is primarily concerned with the actions of the dominant class. The working classes are successfully incorporated by the hegemonic culture of the capitalist class and the whole ideological apparatus of the state bears down upon the subordinate classes, thereby securing the stability of the system as a whole. In short, the critique of reformism tends to assume a dominant ideology thesis in which the working classes are perpetually incorporated and have no significant impact on the development of capitalism. Such a position greatly underestimates the extent of oppositional views in society and the existence of delegitimizing practices on the part of subordinate groups. More importantly, this incorporationist view has to deny any success on the part of the working classes in changing the conditions of capitalist exploitation through the quest for greater social and welfare rights. The working classes are pictured as supine, defeated and subordinated to the overwhelming force of capitalist social structures.

Ralph Miliband (1969), in his original characterization of capitalism in *The State in Capitalist Society*, saw the English working classes as completely dominated by the capitalist-owned mass media, the state system and the local apparatus of government; but in his more recent political sociology, he has detected a widespread desubordination within the general population in a variety of institutional contexts. While desubordination is not equivalent to the development of a revolutionary consciousness, Miliband considers that trade-union consciousness and economistic demands have been far more significant than the critique of reformism typically assumed. Thus he points to the miners' strike of 1972–3 and the campaigns against the Wilson government as setting distinctive limits on the capitalist system, and also noted that the ranks of organized labour now include intellectual workers so that the critique of the existing social structure extends across a much wider social perspective. The consequence of this desubordination is a society characterized by 'continued conflict, antagonistic industrial relations and a climate in which cooperation between the two sides of industry remains as elusive as ever, notwithstanding the objurgations of politicians, prelates and princes. Strike action is an habitual feature of such a situation, and episodically assumes the character of major and de-stabilising confrontations between labour and the state' (Miliband, 1982, p. 152). Any other interpretation of the British situation over the past century has to assume that working-class political activity is inevitably ineffectual and that no significant advances are possible for the working classes without the total destruction of capitalism.

The analysis of capitalism which emerges from the critique of reformism presents a picture of capitalist societies which is far too coherent, stable and lacking in contradictory processes. If the working classes are successful in achieving greater welfare, then this helps the capitalist class to remain in power by pacifying subordinate groups. If the working classes fail to achieve welfare rights, this benefits the capitalist class because the profitability of investment is maximized. There is little room for contradictory pressures inside capitalism in such an analysis. Just as the working classes are regarded as uniformly misdirected by trade-union consciousness, so the dominant class is pictured in a way which is equally over-coherent. The concept of 'ruling class' combines a political notion of authoritarian rule with an economic categorization of class, which fails to distinguish types of dominant class and also fails to consider possible divisions within the dominant class. In practice the so-called ruling class is often constrained in capitalism by the democratic political process and its scope for manoeuvre in economic terms is equally limited in a context of international capitalism. In Great Britain there has been a classic contradiction between industrial capitalism and financial capital, and one role for the state is obviously to stabilize these contradictions by creating some form of social unity. We need to consider these relationships as unresolved contradictions where the interests of the 'ruling class', the interests of workers and other classes, and the political objectives of the state rarely coincide. These contradictory pressures between the demands of the dominant class for economic expansion, the demands of other classes for welfare rights and finally the taxation needs of the state were encapsulated in T. H. Marshall's notion of the 'hyphenated society' where there is a constant and contradictory opposition between these forces producing a society which is inherently unstable and where the scope of desubordination is maximized (Marshall, 1981). In this conceptualization of capitalist society which assumes that there is a disjunction between the political institutions and the economic base, there is no inbuilt assumption about either equilibrium or about social consensus; indeed it is assumed that conflict is the normal state of affairs in a competitive and market-dominated society where the state intervenes to stabilize the conflict between groups but cannot achieve an overall consensus.

Economics and Politics
The critique of reformism and trade-union consciousness is based upon Marx's critique of nineteenth-century political democracy and the objections of Lenin and Luxemburg to revisionism in the early decades of the twentieth century. The critique of trade-union action inside capitalism tends to assume that there has been relatively little change in the character of

capitalism in the advanced industrial societies of Europe and North America. In the nineteenth-century context Marx assumed that the cash nexus was the dominant feature of social relationships and it was this nexus which ultimately subordinated the worker to the control and authority of the owners of productive capital. The subordination of the worker was based on the fact that the labourer was forced to sell his or her labour power in order to survive. In 1985 there were over 3 million unemployed people in Great Britain but there were not over 3 million starving people in Great Britain.

Welfare is not simply an amelioration of the cash nexus; welfare rights have in fact fundamentally transformed this relationship as an outcome of successful class struggle over a period of some hundred years. This change should be seen in the context of a series of structural transformations of capitalist society with the development of so-called monopoly capitalism. It is difficult to read Engels' *The Condition of the Working Class in 1844*, especially the section on the industrial great towns of north-western Great Britain and to read Richard Hoggart's *The Uses of Literacy* (1957) with special reference to Leeds without being fundamentally convinced that the condition of the working classes has improved massively over the past century as an outcome of the struggle for welfare rights. Capitalism by revolutionizing the means of production increased the sum total of wealth with the result that the economic circumstances of the working classes have improved significantly despite the persistence of inequalities in the distribution of this wealth. The working classes clearly do question the way in which these rewards are distributed, but this distribution can be altered substantially without undermining the capitalist mode of production. By comparison with early capitalism, the liberal democratic political system of capitalism has increased the political influence of the organized working classes on the dominant group. These reformist advances may threaten the interests of this dominant class because there is a conflict between the redistributive character of citizenship rights against the profit motive of the free market.

We need to re-think Marx's characterization of capitalism in order to create new possibilities for analysing the relationship between welfare rights, political processes and the economic conditions of capitalist profitability. The critique of reformism largely assumes a direct relationship between the economic base of capitalism and the political manifestations of democracy, such that the economic base directly determines the political manifestations. It is on that basis that the so-called merely political feature of citizenship is regarded as an empty shell, because it does not involve a radical transformation of the economic feature. According to Marxism it is only through a radical transformation of the underlying economic structure that political rights and citizenship can have any real content. In other words the economic base determines the political superstructure. However, it is important to have a perspective on the political feature as a relatively autonomous process with its own effectivity. The political character of capitalism has a very important consequence for working-class struggle but also for the organization of the economic institution of capitalist society. There does not appear to be a direct correspondence between the economic organization of capitalism and its political structure and culture, since capitalism appears to survive under a variety of political regimes ranging from the liberal democratic through to the authoritarian and fascist. To argue that all forms of citizenship in capitalism are a mere sham robs us of the ability to make a distinction between the relatively open political culture of a society like Holland in comparison with the authoritarian political character of South Africa. There may also be important differences within societies which have, for example, a federal political structure so that in Australia there are massive political differences between Queensland and South Australia. These differences play a very important role in working-class politics and cannot be dismissed as a mere shadow of some deeper causal process in the economic structure of society.

The important feature of capitalism is the differentiation of the political from the economic aspects. In principle the market is relatively free from political interventions and the political citizen is differentiated from the economic agent. While this differentiation of the political and the economic aspects is normally discussed within a Marxist vocabulary, it is worth remembering that it was Talcott Parsons who first treated the differentiation of the subsystems of society as the most significant indicator of the process of modernization and social change in capitalist society. For Parsons it was this differentiation of spheres which created a space for the realization of political rights and freedoms on the part of citizens. Because there is a relative separation of the state from the economic institutions of capitalism, governments are not directly held responsible for the operation of the economy. The government is seen to aid or interfere with economic processes but is not held ultimately responsible for all outcomes of economic decision-making. The consequence of this separation is that governments are not automatically destabilized in terms of their political legitimacy when there is a sharp economic downturn. Governments in capitalist society can always claim that international disturbances in the financing of capital or adverse changes in the prices of raw materials are responsible for unemployment or inflation in the home economy. The government therefore does not need to regulate society totally in order to guarantee its continuity and legitimacy. Capitalist governments are thus relatively tolerant of ideological pluralism, personal dissent and opposition (at least within certain boundaries). The consequence of this relative separation of the political and the economic is that the private citizen enjoys a degree of civil rights which is not available in societies where this differentiation has not taken place or in societies where the differentiation has been subordinated. Capitalist governments do not require an overarching dominant or hegemonic ideology; one reason for this is precisely the degree of differentiation of spheres of activity between the economic, the political and the cultural. Parsons' notion of the subsystems of a society can thus be used to explain the relatively low level of value consensus which capitalist government actually requires. The separation of the political and the economic features creates an interstitial space where civil rights of citizenship can be enjoyed. This separation increases the level of inequality in society by giving the economy relative freedom so that there are massive differences in income and wealth, but one consequence of this is a greater enjoyment of civil rights. Capital is relatively indifferent to the beliefs and attitudes of political citizens, because the functioning of economic units does not require an overarching value consensus or dominant ideology.

The situation in planned societies is very different since there is no significant separation of the political and the economic aspects. It is obviously the case that in many so-called socialist societies there is a free market so that the union of the political and the economic aspects is always relative. In planned societies, the state is held responsible for all events which happen within the nation-state. The state is thus vulnerable in situations of economic crisis since the very planning of the economy implies control and control implies responsibility for consequences. The state is relatively intolerant of ideological variation and pluralism, since it requires greater control in both the political and economic realms. It must insist on greater attitudinal and ideological conformity to the system because its political authority is vulnerable via social and economic disturbance. Because there is no or little differentiation between the political and economic features, there is no interstitial space for citizenship. The paradox is that the ideological apparatus of the state has to be expanded in a centralized socialist system whereas late capitalism does not require such massive ideological underpinning because the differentiation of the system allows the state to be 'more tolerant' of individual deviation from the political culture. In capitalism the citizens are more unequal but have a greater range of civil freedoms; in socialism the citizens are more equal, but do not have the same civil rights because the state is vulnerable with respect to economic crises.

It is often assumed that capitalism has specific conditions of existence which must be fulfilled in detail in order for capitalism to survive. We may define capitalism as a system in which there is private ownership and control of the economic means of production, where economic activity is geared to making profits in the framework of a market which regulates economic activity, where profits are appropriated by the owners of capital and where labour is provided by workers who are defined as economically free agents. In practice these conditions of capitalism vary considerably over time and space. Early capitalism or competitive capitalism was characteristic of Great Britain and the USA in the nineteenth century but in the twentieth century there have been significant changes in the nature of ownership, the state's involvement in the economy, the organization of the market and the provision of investment funds. In Australia, for example, over 90 per cent of all wages are fixed by arbitration through centralized administrative units and the Arbitration Commission is responsible for the resolution of disputes over interests. In capitalism generally the state plays an increasingly significant role in the organization of society and there is consequently considerable deviation from the ideal typical characterization of competitive capitalism in conventional economic theory. The individual capitalist running and organizing his own firm has been largely replaced by the multinational corporation or by the state-backed enterprise where there is considerable 'depersonalization' of the characteristic form of economic ownership. In order to survive capitalism does not require an overarching ideology; it does not need incorporated and subordinate working classes since capitalism can survive quite extensive desubordination; it does not require a liberal democratic political system. It is often said that capitalism cannot tolerate real citizenship because this would interfere not only with profitability but with the hierarchical and authoritarian structure of the factory. The growth of real citizenship in the workplace would bring into question the ultimate dominance of the capitalist class. In practice, capitalism is extremely flexible sociologically and does not appear to require such detailed submission and conformity. One explanation of this stability is the high level of structural differentiation in capitalism between the economy and the polity, but also between private and public space, between the workplace and the household. Disturbances in one sector of capitalism do not therefore spill over into the whole social system.

Against Romanticism
If the real advance of the working classes through the expansion of welfare rights is rejected as mere reformism and conformity to the logic of capitalism then anti-reformist politics often assumes a violent character. The development of a revolutionary consciousness will in this analysis require some violent political struggle to undermine the state and to win the working classes as the majority of the population out of its conformity and subordination to capitalist consumerism. Although extra-parliamentary political violence is now a common feature of most industrial

capitalist societies, there is relatively little evidence that these violent practices could in fact undermine a nation-state or that these actions gain much support from the majority of the working classes even where they do not recognize the legitimacy of existing social arrangements for the distribution of wealth. Capitalist political systems are threatened primarily by nationalist, subnationalist or ethnic politics rather than by class confrontation of an extra-parliamentary or violent variety. The drive for regional autonomy or nationalist secession has periodically destabilized Spain, France, Italy and Great Britain, but it is not evident that these nationalist or ethnic movements can be easily incorporated within the theoretical framework of Marxism as revolutionary movements against the dominance of capital.

The critique of reformism conceptualizes the transformation of capitalism in terms of a revolutionary overthrow of the system by class struggle under the leadership of an organized political party. There is a romantic element to this view of politics in contemporary capitalist societies since there is nothing in the structure, history and culture of the working classes which suggests that such a revolutionary event is likely in the advanced industrial societies of the capitalist system. The revolutionary movements of the twentieth century have been more characteristic of the periphery rather than the core of the system and are more likely to take place in the early stages of capitalist development in societies undergoing rapid urbanization. For example, the important revolutionary movements against capitalism in this century have been peasant rather than working-class revolutionary movements (Wolf, 1971). Expanding capitalism in peripheral and rural societies provides the context for revolutionary conflicts, whereas strikes, disruption and industrial conflict are more likely in advanced capitalist systems, where 'explosions of consciousness' give rise to periodic interclass struggle rather than a revolutionary consciousness associated with the imminent overthrow of a social system (Mann, 1973). In modern capitalism the revisionist description of class structure by Eduard Bernstein appears to offer a reliable empirical account of the absence of pauperization and polarization of classes. Technical changes in the nature of production, the changing energy sources of capitalism and changes in the social structure with the growth of welfare have brought about a relative decline in the size of the manual, urban, industrial working classes in contemporary capitalism. The account of the class structure which we find in *The Communist Manifesto* is increasingly irrelevant as an account of the class structure of advanced capitalism and the picture of revolutionary activity in that early pamphlet no longer provides a meaningful characterization of political activity in modern industrial capitalism. By contrast, Marx's later writing on the role of the organized working classes within a parliamentary system is relevant for a discussion of the potentially contradictory relationship between the rapid expansion of welfare rights and the continuity of private profits. Gradual changes in consumption, welfare and the distribution of rights through social engineering are more likely than a revolutionary transformation of the whole social structure. The social role of the romantic revolutionary of the nineteenth century appears to have declined significantly with the advance of urban industrial capitalism. If capitalism is changing these changes are brought about as a consequence of collective resistance and collective pressure to improve welfare conditions and to expand civil rights to minority groups as a consequence of pragmatic and mundane politics. In this context it is empirically difficult to know at which stage reformism slides into radicalism and radicalism slides into revolution. In this situation mass struggle and class confrontation are clearly important in expanding democracy as a principle which is incompatible with private capital accumulation. Political activity in contemporary society requires not the dismissal of bourgeois freedoms as a sham but the utilization of this democratic principle in order to bring into question the dominance of the capitalist class within the political system. In this sense the struggle for citizenship is not a liberal fantasy but a necessary feature of any socialist strategy (Gorz, 1975; Carnoy, 1984).

MARSHALL ON CITIZENSHIP

Marshall provides an attractive theory of social rights in capitalist society which is important on at least five counts (Marshall, 1977, 1981). First, he does not assume a dominant ideology in capitalist society which incorporates the working classes as a subordinate element in the capitalist structure, but on the contrary emphasizes the conflictual role of the working classes in contemporary society. Secondly, he gives full recognition to the real advances achieved by the working classes in the nineteenth century as a consequence of their political and social opposition to the capitalist market place. Thirdly, he provides an interesting framework for the analysis of the history of the working classes in conjunction with an historical view of the evolution of social rights from civil liberties to welfare. Fourthly, he develops a theory of capitalist society which gives adequate recognition to the contradictory and paradoxical forces of capitalist social development, where in particular there is a contradiction between the inequality of class in the market place and the democratic element of citizenship in the political sphere. Fifthly, his analysis of the tension between class and citizenship provides one of the most stimulating frameworks for the analysis of British social policy where policy formation is caught in the contradictory logic of politics versus economics within a democratic political structure (Marshall, 1975).

While Marshall's sociology of welfare capitalism has received appreciative commentary from Lockwood (1974), Goldthorpe (1978) and Halsey (1984), there has also been a critical commentary on Marshall's development on the idea of citizenship by a variety of sociologists. For example, Giddens (1982) criticizes Marshall for holding an evolutionary view of the development of citizenship as though these rights were the immanent development of a social force within society. By contrast, Giddens emphasizes the importance of struggle in the development of citizenship rights. This is not appropriate criticism because Marhall's account of citizenship does not *necessarily* entail some commitment to an immanent logic in capital; on the contrary, his view of citizenship appears to rest on a contingent view of historical development. This view of the importance of struggle was more explicitly developed in his notion of hyphenated society. Giddens also accuses Marshall of ignoring the wider international context within which citizenship develops; in order to win the commitment of the British population in wartime, the British government had to develop a stronger policy on social welfare rights. It is odd that Giddens should criticize Marshall on this issue since Marshall specifically says in his account of social policy that it would be impossible to comprehend British social policy without having an understanding of the impact of warfare on the development of social rights. Giddens goes further to criticize Marshall for treating rights as homogeneous features of citizenship since civil rights which were won by the bourgeoisie are very different from the welfare rights achieved by the working classes. Whereas individual bourgeois rights tend to confirm the dominance of capital through the notion of free labour, welfare rights and other economic rights such as the right to strike appear to contradict the capitalist market. Finally, Marshall is criticized for treating the development of citizenship rights as an irreversible trend of development. While this is a plausible criticism of Marshall, Marshall's actual treatment of historical development is self-consciously in opposition to the evolutionary historical analysis of writers like L. T. Hobhouse and Morris Ginsberg. In *Class, Citizenship and Social Development*, Marshall (1977) specifically rejected the macro-sociology of social change associated with Hobhouse and again, in is writing on demographic history, in practice he did not adhere to an immanent, evolutionary perspective. Certainly, assumptions about irreversible trends are not a necessary feature of his theory and any emphasis on contingent social relationships in social struggle would rule out such a perspective. If we are to criticize Marshall it should be on rather different grounds from those suggested by Giddens.

If citizenship is ultimately about the conditions of social participation, we cannot discuss the notion of national citizenship without considering the constitution of the nation-state. Marshall takes the British nation-state for granted but it is important to bear in mind the problem of the national constitution of the British system. The development of British citizenship involved the decline of Welsh and Scottish civil rights with the increasing dominance of England as the core region. The expansion of social rights in Great Britain to some extent involved, through internal colonialism, the diminution of political participation and regional autonomy in Ireland, Scotland and Wales. Marshall does not really address the problem of how the expansion of social rights within a national core might entail the withdrawal of significant political rights at the periphery. From a celtic perspective, the expansion of the English core state involved the loss of language and religious rights and, more generally, the erosion of celtic culture. In the British case this decline of cultural autonomy was in exchange for participation in the British imperial expansion whereby, for example, Scottish engineers found significant employment in the colonies while the Scottish economy went ultimately into recession. Therefore, we need to discuss citizenship always within the context of national conflicts and colonial development. It can be argued that the accumulation of wealth at the core and the growth of welfare rights in such geopolitical regions was always at the cost of underdevelopment on the periphery. If the growth of English social rights was at the cost of celtic sub-culturalism, there is also a sense in which the expansion of British social rights went alongside the decline of the political autonomy of indigenous populations in the British colonial system. National citizenship thus involved a contradictory relationship between principles of inclusion and exclusion where national identity determines access to economic and political resources. Marshall's argument has to make assumptions about the homogeneity of national populations and even in the British context this assumption was not wholly warranted. Of course, we cannot criticize Marshall on the grounds that his argument does not fit the Lebanese case, for example, but here I merely wish to suggest ways in which his argument could be developed or at least to raise some problems which might arise in the attempt to develop and elaborate his original contribution to the political theory of citizenship.

Another issue raised by Marshall's contribution to the debate concerns the relationship between economic growth and social rights. The period in which he considers the growth of social rights in Great Britain was a period of considerable economic and political development. The growth of wealth provided the cake which was to be divided by the growth of social welfare. Although Great Britain was in *relative* decline by the second half of the nineteenth century there was still considerable economic expansion and this provided the resources which were necessary for some redistribution of wealth. If the most important development of welfare was in the postwar period, then we might note that rising expectations in the 1950s and 1960s were matched by a corresponding increase in productive capacity. It appears then that social welfare rights expand in the context of economic growth but the interesting feature of Marshall's position is that there is a contradiction between social welfare rights and economic growth. More specifically, there are a series of contradictory relationships between the requirement of economic accumulation, commodity consumption and investment in human capital. Marshall's theory was in the last analysis optimistic since he made the assumption that an expansion of social welfare was possible in a capitalist economic context. Contemporary sociologists tend to see the relationship between economic growth and welfare as contradictory, because the expansion of state investment in welfare through taxation places a burden on private profitability. The contemporary problem in Britain is to secure existing welfare rights in a context of monetarism which threatens to undermine working-class social security in an environment of sharp economic decline. While socialist economic theory would suggest that an egalitarian redistribution of wealth in combination with nationalization and protection of local industry would foster the conditions necessary for economic development and expansion, at least in practice societies with a capitalist infrastructure have historically achieved the most significant growth rate in the Third World and many socialist economies are dependent upon significant inputs of western technology and know-how. The high rates of economic growth experienced in societies like Singapore and Japan have not been combined with significant redistribution or a growth in social citizenship. On the contrary, the early stages of capitalist economic growth appear to take place in a context of significant authoritarianism and restrictions on democratic processes.

Another significant change in the British economy since the first publication of Marshall's essay on citizenship is that few individual governments can significantly control and regulate their own economies. The erosion of political and social rights in western capitalism and in other societies in the 1980s is linked necessarily to large-scale global changes in the economy. The growing strength of the American dollar in the 1980s contributed to the erosion of the English economy and the decline in world oil prices meant that the British government could no longer depend upon tax royalties from the North Sea oil exploration to prop up its economic deficit, especially the contributions which were necessary to the unemployed. There was also an important shift in the world economy towards the Pacific basin region away from northern Europe. The point of these illustrations is to suggest that citizenship is not simply a struggle between capital and labour within a national environment and the protection of social rights is not simply a question of the state freely intervening to regulate social relationships. In large measure, modern capitalist governments do not have significant control over their own economies and their commitment to welfare may be very difficult to sustain in a situation where world economic forces are working to undermine nation-state autonomy. The postwar political consensus whereby both the Conservative and Labour parties had converged towards the centre of the political spectrum collapsed under the dual impact of Thatcher's politics and Britain's economic decline in the global capitalist system; this decline in turn stimulated the desubordination of the population since expectations do not decline as quickly as economies. The world in which Marshall originally framed his view of citizenship no longer exists and the economic context which made welfare growth possible has been considerably eroded by recession and global economic change.

CITIZENSHIP AND THE ECONOMY

There are a variety of processes in modern industrial societies which make it difficult to sustain normative status hierarchies. Social and geographical mobility renders traditional rural communities, with their status hierarchies, unstable and delegitimizes sacred authority. The combined processes of urbanization and secularization bring into question the conventional authority of gerontocracy and patriarchy (Gellner, 1979). Mass consumerism also makes available luxuries which in previous generations were restricted to the few. The development of citizenship is one feature, albeit the central feature, of the emerging egalitarianism of modern societies. By arguing that modern societies become less status bound, or at least less committed to formal hierarchies, it is not assumed that economic equality also becomes general. It is simply to argue that traditional social hierarchies in feudalism give way in capitalism to the cash nexus in which no normative authority is given to traditional sources of power. Money becomes the great equalizer while paradoxically leaving market inequalities relatively entrenched. One consequence of these social developments is that it is difficult for governments to appeal to 'responsible' trade unions to restrain the expectations and ambitions of their members in the interests of a moral community. Economism embodies this lack of 'moral' commitment to the status quo and unrestrained economic demands by trade unions are indicative of a decline of authority relationships and status hierarchies. The growth of citizenship through trade-union demands for wage increases and better working conditions can be seen as part of this change in the moral character of capitalism in relationship to previous societies.

A number of writers have sought to link together the development of citizenship, the decline of status hierarchies, the economism of trade unionism, the sharp increase in British inflation between 1970 and 1976, and the crisis of British capitalism in the form of declining profitability (Glyn and Sutcliffe, 1972; Goldthorpe, 1978). Of course, the relationship between these variables is complex and there is no general agreement over the causal mechanisms which produce inflation (Ball and Doyle, 1969). The nature of British inflationary developments also has to be seen within the context of the terms of trade and cannot be explained simply in terms of demand and wage-spirals (Phillips, 1958).

One argument is that inflation is caused by the increase of wage costs relative to productivity; according to the wage-push theory the growth of wages was an important feature of British economic decline in the 1970s where the wage–price spiral was a significant feature of declining profitability. The capacity of unions to push up wages is clearly related to their capacity for collective action and thus with their ability to make effective welfare and social demands on employers. Some features of wage-fuelled inflation were of course unintended consequences of wage drift but at least in the 1970s in Great Britain the inflationary spiral was an outcome of intended and effective union activity. Trade-union strength thus made a significant inroad into company profits, generated an inflationary spiral and eroded the competitive edge of British exported goods in the 1970s (Glyn and Sutcliffe, 1972). Economism as a component of reformism does as a consequence change the nature of capitalism, confirming Marshall's view that class and citizenship have been in direct competition in capitalism. While this interpretation of the crisis of capitalism has been challenged (Gamble and Walton, 1976), it seems unreasonable to deny that the significant increases in real wages in the 1970s had no bearing on the decline of British capitalism (Hirst, 1982). It does not follow, of course, that these advances in the 1970s in terms of real wages were sustained by the British working classes since in the economic recession of the 1980s monetarist policies and high levels of unemployment brought about a significant deterioration in the standard of living of the unemployed and retired sections of the population. In any case, capital typically responds to such pressures by an investment strike or by switching its investment to underdeveloped areas where the cost of labour is low.

CONCLUSION

Critics of reformism typically suggest that capital always has the upper hand and that trade-union activity is either frustrated or leads to further incorporation. It is difficult for such writers to recognize or admit real advances in civil, political and social rights on behalf of the working classes as a consequence of mass movements and organized struggle. This rejection of reformism emphasizes the trade-union mentality of the working classes and pictures the workers as incorporated ideologically within the capitalist system and subordinated by political control and by consumerism. The instrumental attitude of the worker towards wages and the allegedly limited nature of trade-union demands are seen to be manifestations of an underlying political conformity to the dominance of capital. Such a picture of the working classes is politically peculiar since it assumes that they are by definition defeated inside capitalism and it is difficult to see why trade-union activity should not lead to a confrontation with capital of a radical nature. Critics of reformism typically wish to emphasize the role of the party in leading working-class activity but this emphasis also characteristically leads to an elitist theory of politics and knowledge. This characterization of the working classes is also historically dubious since we should by contrast see the political and social advancement of the working classes as consequences of successful and effective social struggle through a variety of means, including trade unionism. As we have seen, the economism which is associated with reformism actually does change the character of capitalism by reducing profitability and forcing companies to restructure their activities. The crisis of profitability also brings about further intervention of the state to stabilize capitalism and this intervention further changes the nature of the relationship between capital and labour. A series of contradictory relationships emerge between taxation and profits, between welfare rights and profitability, and ultimately between the political and economic processes of capitalism. If we regard these demands for economic rights as part of the larger package of citizenship, then the analysis of citizenship rights becomes an important feature of the political economy of capitalism and an essential aspect of the sociological grasp of capitalist development. This analysis of citizenship further contributes to the breakdown of the artificial divisions between political science, economics and sociology. This perspective which is an enlargement of the theory originally put forward by T. H. Marshall enables us to transform and go beyond the limited perspective which is characteristic of dominant ideology theories with their emphasis on working-class incorporation. This development of citizenship is necessarily bound up with the changing character of social struggles and social movements in capitalism; an analysis of social movements takes us well beyond the limited framework which emerges in Marxism from the critique of reformism.

3
Social Struggles

PARADOXES OF PROGRESS

Although social theorists in the nineteenth century were overwhelmed by the evidence of rapid social change, they did not regard this progress in a uniform and optimistic fashion. The issue of paradox and contradiction was prominent in virtually all nineteenth-century social theory regarding progress, social change and development. Utilitarian philosophers were overtly optimistic about the possibilities of social advancement but covertly their social world view was dominated by a pessimistic assumption that the economy would stagnate and the early advantages of industrialization would be lost (Turner, 1974b). In addition, writers like J. S. Mill assumed that the extension of the franchise would bring about a stultifying cultural uniformity, the consequences of which would be a form of Chinese stationariness in matters of morality, taste and intellect. Karl Marx's analysis of capitalism was equally complex in the sense that, while capitalism would bring about the degradation of the worker and the exploitation of the majority of the population under conditions of factory despotism, there was nevertheless a progressive dimension to capitalism which undermined the stability of traditional village life. Capitalist development involved the destruction of traditional culture and the extermination of subordinate groups, but this was progress because it eliminated the particularistic values and institutions of traditional societies. Capitalism had a universalistic tendency and was revolutionary as a mode of production. Capitalism brings societies into world history where history involves, for Marx, essentially the action of self-conscious and practical human beings on their environment (Avineri, 1970). Finally, we can note that Max Weber's view of history was grounded in a central paradox in which the best intentions of social actors always ultimately end in a form of self-destruction and self-cancellation (Turner, 1981). Protestantism unleashed critical thought, freedom from magic, autonomy from the church and the liberation of the individual from tradition and custom, but at the same time pushed western society towards a stultifying conformity under the iron hand of rationalization. The primary metaphor of Max Weber's sociology of modern society was the iron cage which was the final outcome of the process of western intellectualism and scientific enquiry. We might summarize Weber's sociology of fatalism as an argument that the principal virtues of western society result in their self-cancellation in a world dominated by formal reason where people had been reduced to mere cogs in the machine.

Nineteenth-century theories of social change are often seen in terms of a central framework which emphasized social evolutionism and a consistent teleology. Herbert Spencer is thus typically perceived as an evolutionary theorist for whom the transition from military to industrial society was a necessary outcome of the general process of differentiation (Peel, 1971). Of course, Darwinistic biology provided the leading metaphors of many evolutionary conceptions of historical changes with the emergence of modern societies. Social Darwinism in particular provided an evolutionary framework for politics and social policy in American theory (Hofstadter, 1955). Dichotomous forms of thought about social change were also prevalent as in the central notion of a transformation from status to contract (Burrow, 1970).

However, below this overtly optimistic view of evolutionary change in which the powers of the citizen would be enhanced, there was an undercurrent of pessimism and fatalism, especially in the German tradition of sociology where a strong romantic current negated any commitment to the notion of inevitable progress. In Germany, Ferdinand Tonnies' contrast between *gemeinschaft* (community) and *gesellschaft* (society) provided a general view of social change which conceptualized the transformation of traditional society as a decline of culture and individual values (Freund, 1978). Civilization in German thought meant the degradation of an urban industrial society and the liquidation of high culture as the inheritance of the German rational tradition. This pessimistic note was also present in Georg Simmel's notion of 'the tragedy of culture' (Frisby, 1981) and the fatalistic and negative perspective on social change was supremely embedded in Max Weber's notion of the rationalization process (Brubaker, 1984).

Whereas at the beginning of the nineteenth century philosophers like Hegel had conceptualized history as the unfolding of a progressive trend towards human self-consciousness and enlightenment, social theorists at the end of the nineteenth century were typically committed to a negative view of social change and were pessimistic in particular about the autonomy of the individual in a society where uniformity was increasingly prevalent in bureaucracy and economic organization. Whereas the revolutionary changes brought about in France had resulted in the liberation of subject and subordinate groups, such as the Jewish ghetto, the long-term trend of industrialization was seen in terms of an increasing enslavement of citizens under the iron hand of bureaucracy and the centralized state. The pessimism of Friedrich Nietzsche, Max Weber and Georg Simmel was eventually inherited by the Frankfurt School and the critical theorists, especially by writers such as Theodor Adorno, Walter Benjamin and Max Horkheimer (Jay, 1973; Bottomore, 1984a). This legacy of despair can also be located in the work of Georg Lukács for whom the outcome of the German rational tradition was the fascist movement in Europe which embodied a blind technical mind in the service of capitalism. For Lukács, the underlying crisis of western rationalism was manifested in the nihilism and alienation of the modern novel (especially in the work of Robert Musil, Thomas Mann and Franz Kafka). The sense of meaninglessness in such novels was the outward manifestation of the decline of high bourgeoise culture, the emergence of a mass society and the dominance of bureaucratic politics, for which the solution was revolutionary socialism (Lukács, 1964). Contemporary critical theory sees modern capitalism in a negative perspective, so that modern culture is seen to be superficial and trivial, but it is also thought that the culture of modern capitalism is effective in incorporating and subduing the working classes and other radical groups. The hedonism and narcissism of contemporary societies have the consequence of pacifying and incorporating opposition and resistance to capitalist society through a process of mass commodification (Featherstone, 1983).

This critical appraisal of capitalism must, therefore, perceive more neutral or descriptive approaches to contemporary society as either naive or cynical in their assessment of the possibilities of progressive change in contemporary capitalist societies. In particular, the functionalism of American sociology was often seen merely as special pleading on behalf of capitalist interests. Although functionalism, especially as a theory of modernization, appeared to adhere to a one-sided and uniformly bland version of industrial societies, it is possible, of course, to develop functionalism in such a way that the paradoxical and uneven features of development processes can be adequately conceptualized. Indeed, one of the more interesting elaborations of modernity and the modernizing process has been presented in Daniel Bell's *The Cultural Contradictions of Capitalism* (1976). Bell's view of contemporary society has the virtue of focusing on contradictions – that is, on both the positive and negative potentiality of modern development. In this respect, Bell can be said to have recaptured the Marxist view of capitalism as inherently contradictory in its universalistic and regressive forms.

DEVELOPMENT AND DISCONTINUITY

Current paradigms in the sociology of development emerged out of the neo-Marxist critique of functionalist theories of social change which had been the dominant hallmark of research in the 1960s. Sociologists like Daniel Lerner, Bert Hoselitz, Wilbert Moore, Alex Inkeles and Gabriel Almond were criticized for the bland optimism of the proposition that industrial development along western capitalist lines would lead, inevitably, to the modernization of traditional societies in the Third World. For these sociologists, citizenship in the broad sense of social participation became the primary criterion for defining and measuring modernization in underdeveloped societies. Much of the critical opposition to the functionalist paradigm was originally organized around the work of A. G. Frank (1967, 1971). These Parsonian theories of development were rejected on more technical grounds that they embraced unacceptable assumptions about evolutionary change within a teleological framework. Other critics pointed out that functionalism typically ignored the global context of external constraints on internal social development; where development failed to occur, these modernizing failures were seen to be the product of internal flaws in the educational system, or levels of achievement, in the absence of entrepreneurial skills or in the rigidity of traditional institutions (Turner, 1978). By contrast, neo-Marxist theories came to see development as essentially uneven and uncertain. Industrialization could, paradoxically, freeze traditional patterns of culture and structure, conserving pre-capitalist labour relationships and intensifying peasant dependency on landlords and merchants. Indeed, it may be the case that capitalism develops best in peripheral societies on the basis of pre-modern forms of labour which are highly exploitative and hierarchical.

The new paradigms of development theory now emphasized the patterns of 'dependency', 'under-development' and 'backwardness' which could exist alongside advanced capitalist production units and alongside the adoption of high-technology industries (Amin, 1974, 1976). The new wave of development theory, while critical of functionalist paradigms, began to raise theoretical issues which could not be easily accommodated within either old or new Marxism. It is possible to express dependency theory and the concept of 'under-development' within the metaphor of base and superstructure by arguing that the industrialization of the economy as a capitalist system does not mean that the superstructure undergoes a corresponding modernization. Indeed, it is typically the case that capitalism may flourish in a context of highly traditional cultures. The result is that the ideological superstructure (familial patterns, legal organization, ideologies, and political attitudes) stands in a relationship of indeterminacy to economic infrastructures (Abercrombie, Hill and Turner, 1984). In short, the neo-Marxist critique of conventional modernization theory raised a number of issues which are fundamentally problematic within Marxism itself. Part of this theoretical crisis related to the relationship between 'traditional' superstructures and 'capitalist' economies, but it also ranged over the relationship between what we may call 'class-reductionist' and 'mode-reductionist' perspectives (Abercrombie, Hill and Turner, 1980). Evidence for this crisis can be seen in the argument that it is no longer possible to have a *general* theory of development at all, since the peculiarities of individual cases of social development defy easy summary. This solution to the problems of any global theory of development threatens to drive neo-Marxism into an empiricist enquiry into specific case studies – a position which fits oddly with the Althusserian origins of this debate over the mode of production. This theoretical uncertainty is illustrated by the proliferation of quotation marks around such notions as 'developing societies' (Alavi and Shanin, 1982).

There has also been a major change in the context of theories of social development. Sociological pessimism about the prospects for development has been reinforced by the economic recession within the developed nations in the 1970s. It is now clear that the possibility of combining dependency with development, backwardness with growth or economic retardation with modernization is not peculiar to so-called Third-World societies. Regional deindustrialization has been the common fate of many European economies during the contemporary period. First, societies which acquire a capitalist economic sector may not be able to develop in a coherent fashion towards modernization. Secondly, well-established capitalist societies may experience patterns of dependency and deindustrialization which threaten to convert them back into premodern societies. Whereas theorists like Alain Touraine and Daniel Bell had predicted the emergence of the postindustrial society as a consequence of the information revolution, contemporary sociologists of development are more likely to see the future of western industrial societies as one of deindustrialization and deskilling of the working classes, producing poverty rather than affluence. Thirdly, the rationale for a special sociology of developing societies is historically limited, since deindustrialization blurs a geographical distinction which is sociologically highly problematic. The discourse which produced 'oriental societies' and 'occidental societies' is largely redundant and obsolescent (Said, 1978). Sociology simply requires an adequate theory of social change which will address itself to problems of uneven development, discontinuity and contingency.

Whereas conventional theories of social development had a unitary conception of development, recent trends in the analysis of developing societies have emphasized the diversity of the historical pathways to socioeconomic development and they have also argued that there is an enormous variety of developmental outcomes in world history. We might, in addition, draw attention to similar positions which have been taken on the history of western capitalism. First, the historical origins of capitalism in such societies as Great Britain, France and Germany, were very different and hence it is difficult to maintain the view that there is a typical model of the 'bourgeois revolution' (Poulantzas, 1973). Secondly, it is clear that capitalist societies can assume a variety of political shells ranging from fascism to parliamentary democracy and it is certainly not evident that liberalism is the most suitable form of capitalist politics (Jessop, 1978). There is a parallel between these theoretical debates on the nature of western capitalism and those issues in the sociology of development which hinge on the relationship between modernization and industrialization. This parallel might be expressed in the question: to what extent does 'modernization' (the growth of participatory politics, literacy, urbanization, rational administration, egalitarian distribution of wealth and secularization) tend to follow 'industrialization'? In this chapter it is argued that the answer to this question may be located in an extended examination and elaboration of T. H. Marshall's analysis of the contradictory relationships between class and citizenship in hyphenated society (democratic-welfare-capitalism). In this chapter, therefore, I wish to show that Marshall's analysis of welfare capitalism, in fact, opens up a very wide debate about the nature of modernization in relationship to economic expansion, since Marshall's notion of citizenship can be used as the basic definition of modernization.

The relationship between economic development and social modernization is determined by the outcome of variations in class conflict, migration, warfare and ideology on the route out of traditional society. The struggle for citizenship can be seen as a universalistic criterion of social development which is not ethnocentric, teleological or idealist. Furthermore, Marshall's view of citizenship once developed in this direction provides the opposite of Weber's pessimism since Marshall can be interpreted as saying that social violence has the potential for expanding the universalistic definition of the citizen via class confrontation, ethnic conflict and migratory transformations of society.

FUNCTIONAL CIRCLES AND CONTINGENCY

The debate about functionalism in the sociology of development came eventually to raise the question of whether conventional Marxism was also an evolutionary model of change with strong functionalist assumptions (Alexander, 1982). The conventional defence of Marx has normally been based on the assertion that Marx did not, in fact, argue for a set of determinate stages in historical development and also that, especially in his commentary on Ireland, Marx was aware that development under conditions of colonial dependency could bring about underdevelopment. We cannot avoid the conclusion, however, that Marx saw capitalist development as inherently contradictory. Capitalist development requires the iron heel of primitive accumulation which separates the producer from the means of production and primitive accumulation requires the violent separation of the peasant from the land. It was for this reason that Marx argued that 'the history of this, their expropriation, is written in the annals of mankind in letters of blood and fire' (Marx, 1924, Vol. 1, p. 669). At the same time, capitalism is progressive in destroying religious mythology, traditional hierarchies and the vegetative life of the traditional peasantry in the countryside. Thus, in terms of the old slogan, the air of the towns breeds new freedoms. Since Marx also saw Asiatic societies as stagnant and stationary, it was quite consistent for Marx to argue that British imperialism in societies like India would necessarily create a modern infrastructure of railways, administration, litcracy and communications which would galvanize and develop the sociocultural system of the Indian subcontinent. In this process of cruel expansion and exploitation, capitalism had universalistic impulses which liquidated the particularity of traditional societies through the creation of a global system of production, distribution and exchange. The more intense the growth of a capitalist economic base, the greater the possibilities for progressive and universalistic transformations of the social structure (Turner, 1977). Marx's perspective on social development involved a view of the unsteady, uncertain and contingent combinations of economic transformation and social development. For Marx the progressive possibilities of the capitalist mode of production were contingent upon the outcome of class organization and class struggles to realize the opportunities created by the destruction of the old feudal order. In the Indian case, he argued that the realization of these potentialities would require either a revolutionary transformation of Great Britain or the undermining of British colonialism by revolutionary struggle in India. Capitalist economic development can only produce a modernization of the social structure if it is accompanied by the liberating effect of class struggle.

By contrast, functionalist theories of modernization and social change generally lacked any view of development as the contingent outcome of organized social struggle, because they saw modernization effects as an inevitable consequence of the modernization process itself. Thus the 'multiplier model' was a common feature of these theories in which the modernization process expands to embrace the whole society as a coherently modern social system. In modernization theory, urbanization increases literacy and media participation; geographical mobility enhances psychological mobility, which in turn encourages the political participation of citizens. The movement towards a coherent 'participant society' was essentially evolutionary, involving a variety of related political, economic and social processes (Lerner, 1958). Under the assumptions of classical economics, the growth of a capitalist sector siphons off surplus labour in the countryside and, with every new circuit of investment, there are correspondingly increases in wage-labour, wages, consumption and investment (Elkan, 1973). In theories of political modernization, the mobilization of the population to achieve collective goals through the use of political parties and other political institutions was also seen in terms of processual models which were similarly evolutionary in their assumptions. Mobilization in political terms was seen as a cumulative growth of political participation (Apter, 1965).

My argument is that, although participation (or more broadly, citizenship) is a reasonable criterion of social modernization, functionalist versions of modernization suffered from two major difficulties. First, they assumed that there is one rather than many routes to capitalism, whereas historically there appear to be a number of distinctive developmental processes. Secondly, there was no systematic account of divergencies from the modernization model which has to be then treated as either historically specific to certain western societies or merely an ideal type from which empirical divergencies are to be expected. The solution seems to be not to abandon the notion of citizenship participation as a universalistic criterion of modernization but to specify the social and historical conditions which generate different routes to modernity. One element of such a theory is to derive from Marx's view that the nature of the class structure and class conflict during the formation of modern capitalist societies has a major impact on the speed, direction and significance of the forces of modernization which are unleashed by capitalist accumulation. One classical statement of such a position in the modern literature was presented by Barrington Moore in *Social Origins of Dictatorship and Democracy* (1966) and to a lesser extent in *Reflections on the Causes of Human Misery* (1972). Although Barrington Moore does not follow a conventional Marxist analysis of social change, his comparative conceptualization of the class conditions of differential patterns of political change draws implicitly on Marx's analysis of the class basis of revolutionary activity as, for example, in *The Eighteenth Brumaire of Louis Bonaparte* of 1852 (Marx, 1973). Although Barrington Moore has been accused of contaminating Marxism with modernization theory (Burke, 1980), his study of the comparative conditions for the development of either dictatorship or democracy appears to be a significant contribution to a comparative Marxist perspective which has stimulated a number of significant inquiries in contemporary sociology (Skocpol, 1979). In any case, part of my argument is that modernization theory can be adequately salvaged once it is disconnected from its original evolutionary presuppositions.

Barrington Moore's explanation of divergent paths to modern society is well known and seminal in contemporary social history and historical sociology. He distinguished between three primary and alternative forms of social change (democratic, fascist and communist) which will account for the very different forms of social structure and political process in England, Germany, France, Japan, China and the USA. These differences were predominantly the product of alternative combinations of class relationships (especially between landlord and peasant) in the formation of post-feudal societies.

In Great Britain, the peasantry as a distinctive class disappeared (through land enclosure) long before the beginning of industrialization and capitalism developed on the basis of an alliance between agrarian–capitalist landlords and an urban mercantile bourgeoisie. The English route to capitalism was subsequently gradualist and democratic, partly because the failure of English absolutism had witnessed the rise of parliamentary forms of political expression, which provided an institutional framework for the growth of citizenship. This aspect of Barrington Moore's analysis has been subsequently extended by a variety of historians who have emphasized the peculiarities of English class history (Anderson, 1974). By contrast, revolutions from above (as in the German case) which depend on massive state intervention in the economy and civil society promote the conditions which lead towards a fascist path to capitalism. It was this aspect of German social history after Bismarck which occupied a large part of Max Weber's political sociology in which Weber saw strong charismatic leadership as one condition for breaking the dominance of bureaucracy and the mass party machine (Eden, 1983). Peasant-based revolutions (as in China) provide some of the necessary conditions for developments toward a communist political framework and a socialist trajectory. Barrington Moore saw these alternatives as historically linked, since the bourgeoise democratic and fascist revolutions create social conditions globally which make communist revolutions both possible and likely. The theory thus argues that the development of democratic political systems involves 'a long and certainly incomplete struggle to do three closely related things: (1) to check arbitrary rulers, (2) to replace arbitrary rulers with just and rational ones, and (3) to obtain a share for the underlying population in the making of rules' (Moore, 1966, p. 414). In the American case, the pathway to democratic institutions was violent, disruptive and uncertain, but as a consequence of the Civil War the dominance of the pastoral landlords was finally broken in the south, liberating Negroes within the political structure of America as a whole. This revolution was obviously incomplete and the status of Negroes as citizens was not fully developed until much later. Indeed, much of the reconstruction after the Civil War led to a re-assertion of the authority of the southern plantocracy through repressive and regressive legislation (Berger, 1967). Although these specific details of Barrington Moore's account can be questioned, his framework establishes criteria for a comparative study of modernization which is grounded in an analysis of class relationships and which does not assume a steady evolutionary emergence of democratic citizenship.

We can see the democratic process as the struggle to destroy premodern forms of absolutism, particularity and despotism; this struggle inevitably involves an attempt to transform patriarchal relationships within the family, the economic exploitation of children, the persistence of archaic and particularistic forms of social relationships, the continuity of religious doctrine of a supernatural variety, and the rigidity of hierarchical subordination on ascriptive criteria. In short, democratic modernization expands the boundaries of civil society to embrace citizens on an egalitarian basis. This is not an evolutionary process since it is dominated by certain contingent relationships of a class nature and the long-term survival of citizenship cannot be guaranteed on a teleological basis.

CLASS, WAR, MIGRATION AND IDEOLOGY

In this chapter it is argued that T. H. Marshall's conception of citizenship can be elaborated and combined with Barrington Moore's historical analysis of democracy to develop an historical and global framework for conceptualizing the development of universalistic citizenship. Further, it is claimed that this framework avoids the pitfalls of functionalism and evolutionary theories of social change, by emphasizing the contingent features of social struggle which have no necessary historical logic or unfolding process. Although Marshall was primarily concerned to use the concepts of citizenship and class to explicate the nature of

British social history, his treatment of the development of British society in terms of the expansion of rights through struggle can be transposed to the debate over development, underdevelopment and dependency in a broader context. The development and modernization of any society can be seen as a struggle to establish citizenship rights of egalitarian membership within a common community. Where these struggles are effective they have the consequence of destroying or weakening particularistic criteria of social value so that age, sex and ethnic identity no longer serve as *principles* of social exclusion. In fact, such particularistic criteria may still account for massive empirical inequalities in income, education and prestige, but such inequalities are attacked and questioned on the grounds that they cannot, in principle, be rationally justified. Isaiah Berlin was generally right in assuming that we now live in societies where it is inequality, not equality, which requires justification. State legislation on sexual discrimination, inherited wealth and discrimination in employment would be obvious examples of this argument. Social particularism becomes the site of popular struggles to challenge in the name of universalistic citizenship the empirical inequalities which exist in the economic market. Of course, this is no guarantee that such struggles will be effective and Ernest Gellner is correct to note that while democracy is universally accepted as a valid norm, its concrete implementation is inversely related to its success as a norm of political legitimacy (Gellner, 1974). Although the outcome of such processes is historically contingent, the dominance of these conflicts in the modernization of societies can hardly be denied or overlooked.

This theme of universalistic citizenship as the central criterion of modernization provides a context for uniting a number of diverse perspectives and approaches in classical and contemporary sociology. To some extent, Marx's view of the liberating impact of capitalist colonialism on traditional societies was an extension of Hegel's notion of history as the unfolding of consciousness against the blinkered reality of tradition, but for Marx this approach was one under conditions of violence. For Marx, the accumulation of wealth under capitalism had an iron heel which represented the expropriation and exploitation of the peasantry in order to provide a surplus for investment in industrial enterprises. This also explains the apparent irony of Engels who welcomed the advance of French colonialism in North Africa because he assumed it would undermine the traditional barbarism of tribal Africa (Tuner, 1978). For Weber, modern politics involved a conflict between the substantive claims of the working classes for social justice and the formal–rational requirements of a legal machine which could not conceptualize justice as a moral issue (Turner, 1981, 1982). The process of rationalization can also be seen as a process which is inimical to particularistic definitions of persons, which are in principle irrelevant to bureaucratic decision-making. Bureaucracy and rational law tend to undermine the particularity of the individual through a process of routinization and individuation which make administrative regulation possible. For Durkheim, one major source of social conflict and a sense of injustice between classes was the survival of inheritance *ab intestat* by which property is distributed and conserved through the family on the particularistic accident of birth. These legal arrangements were seen by Durkheim to be archaic and morally unjustified (Durkheim, 1978). For Talcott Parsons, development was approached via the perspective of the pattern variables and he argued that the test of modernity was the presence of universalistic and achievement norms over particularistic and ascriptive ones. Thus for Parsons the problem of fascism in Germany was that, while in political terms a democratization of society had been evolved, there were still many features of an old hierarchical, rural and patriarchal society in existence (Parsons, 1942). Similarly, Parsons identified the absence of political rights among the American Negroes as incompatible with the general development of a universalistic norm of political membership in the USA as the most advanced and modernized of the industrial societies of the west (Parsons and Clark, 1966).

If universalistic citizenship is thus a reasonable criterion of modernization, then the routes or conditions of citizenship during the process of modernization and industrialization determine the character of modern societies. If citizenship is the outcome of struggle, then the precise nature of these struggles is crucial in shaping the kind of modernization which societies ultimately acquire. In classical Marxism, class struggle was obviously central in determining the nature of political and social life. To give a specific illustration, Perry Anderson has argued that the continuity of a traditional culture in British life was a consequence of an alliance between the urban bourgeoisie and the land-owning aristocracy which had developed as an agrarian capitalist class through the wool industry (Anderson, 1964). The survival of traditional elements in French social structure was an outcome of the survival of the peasant class after the French Revolution (Poulantzas, 1973).

However, both Marxism and sociology have been overoccupied with class analysis to the neglect of other components of modern social change such as war and migration which I shall argue are crucial determinants of the form of modernity. Marxism along with sociology was critically concerned with class formation because it sought to understand the nature of modern capitalism as an outcome of the collapse of feudal society. Of course, a number of important modern societies had no feudal background and were largely the outcome of settler capitalist development and migration. The most interesting examples of settler capitalism from the point of view of modernization would include North America, Australia and New Zealand (Kettner, 1978; Denoon, 1983). While societies like Australia acquired a conservative culture as the inheritance of pastoral capitalism, it did not inherit the dead weight of a traditional feudalism and the transition to modern capitalism was thus very different from the transformative processes of Europe.

The argument of this chapter is that radical citizenship is the outcome of class struggles, war, migration and egalitarian ideologies. Where all four components are present in the modernization of society citizenship is real and expansive rather than formal and defensive. The hypothesis is that where modernity is shaped by all four components then modernity takes a definite radical direction. The converse is that traditional (or particularistic) institutions and practices, which are inconsistent with egalitarian citizenship, secularism, democratic parties and universalistic values, are conserved where these components are more or less absent. Societies which acquire an industrial basis without social modernization through class conflict, migration, warfare and egalitarian ideologies will retain an overarching social structure which is inherently traditionalistic and particularistic. The value of the approach can be illustrated by a variety of historical examples and, in the process of providing these illustrations, it will be important to consider 'divergence' routes to modernization.

Sociologists have traditionally regarded class formation and class conflict as the major dimensions of social change and of the formation of modern consciousness. To some extent Marx provided the starting point for this analysis in drawing a contrast between the fragmented consciousness of the isolated and self-sufficient peasantry and the revolutionary consciousness of the organized, concentrated proletariat within the capitalist enterprise. Through their opposition to capitalist conditions of work, supervision and control, the working classes are welded together as a potent form of opposition. In terms of the arguments being developed here, we could suggest that the mobilization of the working classes as a collectivity with a distinctive consciousness of its class position in opposition to dominant forms of power and exploitation is a necessary condition for the realization of expanded citizenship rights. Marx's original formulation of this dimension of class relationships has of course been much refined by subsequent debate (Parkin, 1972; Mann, 1973; Bottomore, 1975). There are a number of modifications of this original Marxist thesis which are significant. First, we can consider working-class consciousness as a continuum between a sense of class identity, class opposition, class totality and a revolutionary conception of an alternative society. Progression along the continuum may depend upon a variety of factors: the institutionalization of industrial conflict, the presence of radical political organizations, the degree of unionization, the fragmentation of the working classes, the presence of a reserve army of labour, the embourgeoisement of workers and the rate of unemployment, de-skilling and feminization of the labour force (Dahrendorf, 1959; Abercrombie, Hill and Turner, 1980; Littler, 1982). Secondly, it is argued that the working classes are more radical in the early rather than the later stages of industrialization, because recently uprooted rural workers experience alienation more intensely (Wolf, 1971; Cohen, Gutkind and Brazier, 1979). Thirdly, where working-class exploitation is, as it were, over-determined by discrimination on the basis of ethnicity, the radicalization of workers may be more intense. However, most studies of migrant workers see the migrant as embittered but subdued and it is also thought that migrants face great difficulties in forming workers' associations and are co-opted by existing trade unions (Rex, 1970; Zubaida, 1970). In general, it is argued that urbanization, unionization and work experience in large productive units tend to produce class-conscious working classes which are organized to achieve greater participation in society and a wider distribution of social rewards via the acquisition of expanded citizenship. The net effect of these processes is to modernize consciousness so that traditionalist attitudes and practices are transformed and expectations for social reform are magnified.

Against this class-centred view of the modernization of consciousness, it can be argued that aspirations for an expansion of citizenship rights are typically realized in a context of wartime conflict. Whereas Marxists have focused almost exclusively on class conflict as the harbinger of modernity, many of the major advances in the social rights of workers in western society have been consequences of or closely related to warfare. We can distinguish two sets of circumstances in which wartime experiences expand social rights. In the first, the crisis of warfare in the domestic arena creates a situation where dominant social groups are forced to offer an expansion of social rights to the working classes in order to secure and enhance working-class commitment to warfare. Secondly, there are popular war confrontations especially against colonial powers which have the consequence of modernizing consciousness and increasing social participation in decision-making activities. For example, in the first set of circumstances the expansion of women's rights was closely tied to their entry into the work force during the First and Second World Wars. Similarly, advances in housing, education, social security, national insurance and medical provision were a consequence of bargains developed between labour and capital under the auspices of extended state intervention in wartime conditions. Most aspects of state-dominated social security schemes are direct consequences of wartime conditions (Leuchtenburg, 1963; Titmus, 1963; Brown, 1972; Glynn and Oxborrow, 1976).

Warfare reduces unemployment, stimulates the provision of health services and generates a housing shortage which forces the state to intervene and to assume greater responsibility for social welfare. Although warfare necessarily changes social policy, 'the nature of this effect will depend to a considerable extent on the fortunes of war – on whether a country is invaded or not, on whether it is victorious or defeated, and on the amount of physical destruction and social disorganisation it suffers' (Marshall, 1975, p. 82). The consequences of the Second World War for Great Britain and Holland were thus radically different.

War, like class struggle, galvanizes protest and resistance at the same time that it promotes sentiments of patriotic unity, at least in conditions of a popular war against fascism. The combination of patriotism and working-class solidarity is a potent condition for the realization of the rights of citizenship. In addition, occupation during wartime may radicalize consciousness, advance the cause of women as participants in struggle and question the pre-bellum distribution of wealth and privilege. War tends to promote sentiments of patriotic solidarity around questions of participant citizenship as against class-dividing experiences of economic growth. The social effects of terrorism and violence may, however, point in the opposite direction (Worsley, 1972).

Both war and military occupation tend to erode conventional patterns within the sexual division of labour, patriarchy within the family, the dominance of traditional religion and the privilege of conventional status grounded in inheritance and social custom. Wars of liberation and resistance tend in particular to transform the conventional position of women in the society, giving them a new freedom and authority in social relationships. The unintended consequences of militarism are paradoxically beneficial to the development of citizenship rights. However, these wartime advances are often undermined in the aftermath of war as traditional arrangements and power combinations are restored by an alliance of trade unions, business and government. The attempt to minimize the advances achieved by women in the postwar period in Europe is a characteristic illustration of this regressive tendency (Lewenhak, 1980). Although few sociologists have recognized the validity of the argument, external war may promote and crystallize citizenship rights as forcefully as internal wars. Above all, sociology lacks a theorist of war and militarism in a situation where internal conflict (usually conceptualized in terms of class struggles) constitutes the dominant paradigm. In particular, involvement in organized violence appears to promote citizenship for women more than any other single factor. This is not, of course, an argument in favour of apocalyptic politics in the tradition of Georges Sorel's *Reflections on Violence* (Sorel, 1961) but is simply an argument to suggest that social change may owe more to external war than to internal class conflicts.

The third ingredient of revolutionary change promoting struggle for citizenship rights is migration. Here we can distinguish between two different situations. First is the migration of male workers out of traditional rural cultures and the radicalization of urban workers through the experience of geographical and social mobility. Migration from rural to urban centres has the effect of weakening family ties, stimulating individualism and weakening the control of the church over urban populations (Simmel, 1968). Rural migration tends to disrupt the stability of traditional moral communities rendering religious belief especially difficult (MacIntyre, 1967b). Migrants in search of urban employment enter a market-dominated society where cultural pluralism and ethnic diversity contribute to a greater universalism and tolerance of differences (Smith, 1973). The second type of migratory situation is the case of a society (typically Commonwealth society) which is constituted by the fact of migration.

The contradictory features of individual migration have been widely recognized and discussed in sociological studies of migration (Jackson, 1969; Castles and Kosack, 1973; Lacey and Poole, 1979; Martin, 1981; Glazer, 1983). Although the formation of ghettos and the separation of minority groups from the mainstream of social activity tend to neutralize the potential for change in migration, the preservation of traditional cultures in second- and third-generation migrants is notoriously difficult. The radicalization of populations as a result of migratory experience will depend on the type and causes of migration. Where migration is brought about by aspiration to improve standards of living by changing traditional patterns of life, migrants tend to be an innovative and radical community (Petersen, 1958). There are, of course, a variety of other variables which are crucial in this context. When migrant communities suffer social exclusion as a minority group, there may be strong pressures towards popular struggles for citizenship rights. In addition, where villages are feminized as a result of the migration of male workers, women are able to enter leadership and work roles previously preserved for men. Although conservative forms of migration which seek to preserve traditional values and institutions are common, migration is a potentially radical component of social change. More importantly, societies which are actually constituted by migration are typically modern societies (Canada, Australia, New Zealand and Hong Kong) because cultural pluralism is a potent corrosive of established attitude, exclusiveness and particularity. For example, in Hong Kong where 98 per cent of the population is Chinese in place of origin, migration and urban concentration have destroyed much of the traditional village and peasant culture of the Chinese as patriarchal structures have been eroded in the new settlement towns (King and Lee, 1981). Clearly, whether or not the melting pot of ethnicity actually results in progressive social change will depend on contingent circumstances which are political, social and juridicial (van der Berghe, 1983).

The connection between nation building, progressive politics and innovative migration has been most forcefully expressed by Shlomo Avineri with respect to modern Israel. Avineri's thesis is that Jewish settlement of Palestine was 'unique as a form of downward social mobility' and this migration transformed the Diaspora petty bourgeoisie into an Israeli working class (Avineri, 1970). Israel is a genuinely modern society because it has combined secular nationalism in politics with a radical social revolution which is essentially democratic. A similar argument has been developed by Anthony Smith to the effect that modern Israel represents a successful transformation of a religious movement into secular nationalism within a unified policy (Smith, 1973).

This argument has to confront three major problems. First, there is much about the cultural basis of secularism and the state of Israel which is inherently religious (Turner, 1984a). Secondly, the confrontation with the indigenous Palestine population has driven Israel into an exclusive national community (through the law of return) which is incompatible with secular universalism. Thirdly, the Avineri argument would have to be expanded to include the forced migration of Arabs out of Palestine to form a political movement which is characterized by a high degree of revolutionary consciousness. The bitter paradox is that Palestinians now represent a highly educated, mobile and politically conscious global Diaspora (Sayigh, 1979; Zureik, 1979). Settler capitalism (Israel, South Africa and Northern Ireland) often results in a colonial situation where class and racial domination may be intensified, but the intensification may be masked by the adoption of modern means of control (Greenberg, 1980). The lesson to be learnt from these empirical examples is that the modernizing thrust of innovative migration may be deformed where the settler colony encounters an indigenous population sufficiently large and organized to present a threat to the political hegemony of settler migrants. The resistance of black Africans to white supremacy resulted in a violent race-relations situation dividing black and white communities into warring factions. The consequence of such situations was a deformation of the democratic trajectory but clearly ideological factors also play a significant role in legitimizing such racial inequality. In particular, calvinistic Christianity was mobilized by the Dutch reformed church to provide at least one religious backing for apartheid as a system of legitimized racial inequality.

The fourth condition for the development of universalistic citizenship as a component of the process of modernization in the emergence of capitalist societies is the presence of an ideology of egalitarianism and universalism. The nature of the contribution of ideology to either social change or social coherence is difficult to specify (Abercrombie, Hill and Turner, 1980). For example, contemporary India has a constitution which places great emphasis on universalistic equality but in India the caste system has survived modernization, the development of a modern education system and extensive legislation of rights (Béteille, 1983). Ideologies may be regarded as resources which can be mobilized by oppositional groups to bring about change and mobilized by established groups to legitimize the status quo. However, the presence of a strong doctrine of egalitarianism and universalism is an important component in the resources of oppositional groups in their conflict with existing social arrangements. There are two features of ideology which are important in this situation. The first is the view of history which is entailed by any given ideological system and the second is its conceptualization of the basis of social membership.

It can be argued that belief systems with a linear view of history lend themselves more easily to radical social movements than views of history which emphasize circular patterns and doctrines of return. In general, millenarian belief systems have proved to be historically radical in their challenge to the existing social system by offering the promise of a new social order after a period of conflict and struggle (Desroche, 1979). Millenarian movements reject the present order in favour of a radically new society to be brought about by the return of a Messiah and such messianic beliefs were prevalent in the Judeo–Christian tradition; such belief systems, while being vague about the means of social change, stimulated a variety of religious and secular revolutionary movements in adopting a utopian world view which is inimicable to the present order (Hobsbawm, 1959). Although Marxism typically rejects religious radicalism as simply the opium of the people, Marxists also recognize that Christianity provided a model for secular radicalism. Engels' analysis of the peasant insurrections of Germany provided the typical Marxist approach to religious radicalism since Engels claimed that the religious wars of the Reformation were in fact class wars disguised in the language and practice of existing religions (Engels, 1965). These particular interpretations of religious radicalism miss the important issue, which is that in the contemporary period religious faith has provided an essential ingredient of anti-colonial enthusiasm and a major ideological feature of wars of independence since religion provides one of the most potent critiques of alien domination. Religion can thus play an important part in the development of political citizenship which embraces the whole population in a struggle for autonomy and independence.

A second feature of religious ideology is that it provides a universalistic basis for membership in a political community on the basis of faith rather than kinship or locality. The so-called Abrahamic faiths have been significant in this respect since they offer a general basis for the evolution of universalistic notions of political identity. In particular, Christianity and Islam developed eventually on the basis of the notion of universalistic brotherhood. Judaism recognizes egalitarian membership within the Jewish community but Christianity and Islam as missionary religions spread eventually on the basis of a wider and more universalistic notion of membership through faith and ritual conformity. These religions did of course make distinctions between women and races but, at least in principle, membership was on a universalistic criterion. Membership within the universalistic Church or in the case of Islam within the universalistic House of Islam offered the precursor to the notion of a universalistic polity embracing people of radically different ethnic, cultural and social backgrounds. Although in practice neither religions achieved this universalism, they did provide an ideology which minimized the significance of kin and tribal affiliations. This interpretation was crucial, for example, to Talcott Parsons' interpretation of the transformative significance of the Christian notion of universalistic salvation, and Parsons noted that the separation of politics and the sacred in Christianity along with its openness ultimately to denominational differentiation provided the basis for a secular development of pluralistic politics within a policy which assumed a universalistic franchise (Parsons, 1963). Parsons' interpretation of the evolutionary significance of Christianity is, of course, much debated; but the issue which Parsons derives from Max Weber is important for the debate over the origins of egalitarianism as a value. Parsons following Weber argued that theodicy is a radical component of the Christian world view in which, given that all men are equal in the sight of God, how can inequality be justified? In principle, such a theodicy can always take a radical turn and provide the basis for social mobilization to achieve greater equality between citizens conceptualized in a universalistic framework (Turner, 1981).

INDUSTRIALIZATION WITHOUT MODERNIZATION

The argument is that the industrialization of the economy under capitalist conditions can take place without a modernization of the social structure, since modernization (in the sense of an expansion of citizenship rights) is an effect of collective struggles, which are themselves shaped by class structure, warfare, migration and ideologies of equality. Two prominent examples of industrialization without cultural modernization would be Great Britain and Japan which have achieved capitalist development in the absence of a revolutionary transformation of their social structure and culture. There is a wide agreement that the dominant characteristic of modern British history is its gradualism and absence of revolutionary politics. The explanation is commonly that the class alliance of an agrarian capitalist and urban merchant class in the period of capitalist formation has rendered modern Great Britain a traditional society in which monarchy, elitism, established religion, status hierarchies, the old-boy network, racism and traditional values have survived in the face of urbanization and industrialization (Anderson, 1964; Burrage, 1969; Miliband, 1969). Great Britain has entered the modern world with much of the cultural baggage of hierarchical feudalism intact and the sense of the rightness of hierarchical authority has hardly been challenged in contemporary Great Britain. Where there has been a movement for egalitarian citizenship, this has been largely the consequence of popular struggles under conditions of mass mobilization in wartime. Migration in Great Britain has not been a significant factor in transforming British society into an ethnic melting pot or a society characterized by multiculturalism but has instead fragmented working-class opposition to recession. In addition, the long pattern of internal colonialism has often divided oppositional politics along regional and subnational lines (Hechter, 1975; Hayward and Berki, 1979). The British cultural superstructure has not been transformed or destroyed by invasion, by massive migratory waves, by a radically egalitarian doctrine or by a class confrontation of a revolutionary kind. The consequence is that while in many repects Great Britain has enjoyed a period of liberalism and an expansion of citizenship its hierarchical and particularistic culture has survived industrialization. In this sense Great Britain is not a modern society.

A similar argument can be mounted with respect to Japanese society. Japan industrialized without a major reconstitution of centralized feudalism by either a peasant or a bourgeois revolution. Japan had no history of autonomous cities within which a thriving mercantile, burgher culture could develop. There has been no important experience of migration, leaving Japan with an homogeneous population with a distinctively chauvinist attitude towards outsiders. Industrialization was undertaken not in opposition to but with the aid of such traditional values as loyalty to the Emperor and filial piety within the family (Saniel, 1965). Although the reforms achieved under the allied occupation were important, much of Japanese traditional institutions survived both economic industrialization and military defeat. One dominant feature of the society is the persistence of vertical systems of stratification based on personal contacts, on loyalty rather than the emergence of horizontal class relationships based on impersonal economic relationships (Nakane, 1973). Although Japan's involvement in war had the effect of stimulating its economic development during the period of contemporary modernization, the army and navy in Japan, unlike their role in other societies, have contributed to the stability of traditional relationships and emphasized primary personal contact rather than bureaucratic and neutral social organization (Ike, 1973). While urbanization and changes in the educational curriculum have done much to create a mobile and egalitarian culture, traditional values relating to the family, to religion and to the authority of the firm have survived these changes in social structure. By comparison with other so-called modern societies, Japan has retained much of its premodern culture and organization (Dore, 1958, 1967). The absence of a strong and widespread egalitarian citizenship norm is probably best illustrated by the very negative attitude of Japanese towards outcasts (the *burakumin*) and by Japanese attitudes towards foreigners (who are generally designated as barbarians).

Both Japan and Great Britain thus form a definite contrast to societies like Canada, Australia and New Zealand. Although these Commonwealth countries were founded on the assumption of the white, protestant ascendancy, their migrant development has largely eroded the possibility of an imposed cultural uniformity (Hartz, 1964; Tatz, 1972; Price, 1974). These colonial societies had no feudal background and were constituted by waves of white migration. Although Australia has a peculiar distinction of being created as a convict settlement, its development was made possible by largely voluntary, innovative migration by Europeans (and more recently by Asians) in search of improved standards of living and in some respects greater political freedom. Neither Canada nor Australia has a history of violent class struggle, but there is a considerable record of working-class militancy and protest (Connell and Irving, 1980). While both societies have a long record of racism, the indigenous Aboriginal population has never been separated by a pattern of institutional and legitimate apartheid. Aboriginal populations in these societies have long been excluded from the central mechanisms of citizenship, but in recent years the struggle for land rights has done much to galvanize these indigenous groups and create the conditions for a transformation of their legal status. In short, these settler societies were developed as agrarian capitalist systems on the basis of migrant work forces within the framework of a parliamentary democracy in which political and civil rights were established relatively quickly. This is not to argue that societies like Australia are wholly egalitarian or lack significant class divisions; these colonial societies like others have well-established patterns of systematic inequality (Porter, 1965; Western, 1983). Canada and Australia have achieved economic development alongside a modernized social system which is secular, multi-cultural and relatively egalitarian. They have been relatively successful in establishing general social rights for citizens regardless of their ethnic origin. This is a valid argument despite the fact that there is much de-facto discrimination against new migrants and despite the presence of quite distinctively racist ideologies (de Lepervanche, 1984).

IDEOLOGY, MINORITY STATUS AND THE STATE

It has been argued that modernization can be defined in terms of the growth of citizenship rights and that these rights are the outcome of collective struggles to preserve or to enhance membership within a community, that is to be recognized as bona fide members of a nation-state. The history of citizenship will in part be a history of the state as that institutional framework within which citizenship can operate. The 'citizen' is bound up with the evolution of both *civitas* and 'civility', that is with the growth of the city and with civilization. The relationship between citizens is essentially political and contractual and thus unlike feudal relationships of an hierarchical and personal variety. Citizens are not necessarily kinsmen and we might argue that the political ties of citizenship are actually incompatible with the particularistic blood ties of either real or fictive kinship. Citizens are individuals in a political relationship which is at least formally universalistic within the confines of the state. A number of writers, especially Lucian Goldmann (1973), have suggested that the notions of contract, individualism and universalism were principal components of Enlightenment thought developing with the expansion of exchange relationships, markets and urban centres. Although the notion of egalitarian citizenship and political participation has a specific relationship to bourgeois capitalist culture, the notions of individualism and universalism are clearly much older and have their roots in both Stoicism and Christianity. Although Weber made no direct contribution to the debate about citizenship, it is important to consider Weber's view on the revolutionary impact of Christian universalism, on the development of the city and thus by implication on modern citizenship.

It appears that the growth of an autonomous urban culture with independent burghers is one precondition for the emergence of both individualism and citizenship. Citizens are essentially not rural dwellers and the growth of universalistic rights requires the decline of strong kinship ties and a doctrine which can conceive of social relationships which are not blood relationships. For Weber, Christian universalism was the precondition for the notion that persons are bound together by belief rather than by descent. The historical importance of Christianity was that it 'deprived the clan of its last ritualistic importance, for by its very nature the Christian community was a confessional association of believing individuals rather than a ritualistic association of clans' (Weber, 1958, p. 103). A number of paradoxes follow, however, from this revolutionary doctrine. It is inevitable that a universalistic creed should produce particularistic consequences in the form of sects, heresies and deviances. Against the church, there is always the sect, because orthodoxy creates the antidote of heresy. The boundaries of membership within the confessional association are defined by an anti-group of nonmembers. Indeed, one consequence of Christian universalism was to constitute, as Weber recognized, the Jews as a pariah-people (Stammer, 1971). This Christian association of believers created an anti-group of unbelievers which required the lines of demarcation to be controlled by political restraint. The problem for Christianity was its apolitical character and hence the boundaries of membership required the state as an institution of legitimate violence (Turner, 1976). The consequence of this relationship was a politicization of the Church in which political membership of the state came to be coterminus with doctrinal membership within the religious association. Eventually with a secularization of the universal Church and the arrival of national churches, political citizenship predominated over spiritual membership. The passport rather than baptism was the defining characteristic of communal membership. An alternative view has been that modern societies require a 'civil religion' to mitigate the divisive forces of class status and power (Robertson, 1978). The social consequences, however, are relatively unchanged. Any attempt to create citizens on the basis of one criterion of sameness (whether that criterion is based on language, religion, culture or belief) generates – or at least identifies – differences. Minority status is therefore never a purely statistical or numerical phenomenon but is a condition created by ideological definition of normality, since membership always defines antimembership. Witchcraft trials, whether they are conducted on religious or political premises, are attempts to define boundaries of inclusion–exclusion (Hepworth and Turner, 1982). Indeed, society as such can be conceptualized as the outcome of such rituals of inclusion and exclusion.

The other paradox of Weber's account of Christian universalism is its relationship to Judaism and Islam. In general, the

Abrahamic faiths were monotheistic, prophetic, literary and eschatological. Although Weber argued a counter-position, it can be suggested that Islam is more universalistic and rational than Christianity, and furthermore Islam is a unified religio-political association. Although Judaism was originally a tribal confederacy united by a covenant, the motif of political restoration has been the dominant influence on Jewish history in the conditions of the Diaspora (Sharot, 1976). The important point is that, while these Abrahamic faiths have much in common, they were mutually exclusive, because creedal universalism precluded institutional tolerance towards minorities which also claimed universalism on the basis of the truth of their beliefs. That is, it is difficult to conceive of two universalistic religions cohabiting within the space of a single political framework. Universalistic faiths which are excluded from the dominant culture and forced into minority status are thus faced with a limited number of options (Deshen and Zenner, 1982). They may assimilate to the local culture by minimizing their public differences: intermarriage is thus a prominent mechanism of assimilation and syncretism. They may privatize their faith so that belief and observance become a matter of individual preference within the domestic sphere. Finally, minority status may give rise to more or less permanent subgroups which retain their identity at the cost of significant social influence. They perform 'dirty work' on behalf of the dominant group in exchange for their subnational continuity. These groups are, so to speak, permanent sects. Such minority groups often remain 'frozen' in traditional patterns, beliefs and rituals, avoiding the secularization and modernization experienced by the host community. One example of this freezing of cultures is the history of traditional Sephardic Jews in North African Arab societies which did not experience significant secularization or modernization until their eventual migration to modern Israel where they are forced to adjust to radically different social circumstances.

Minorities are ideological not arithmetical entities. For example, from the point of view citizenship as the criterion of social membership, women were a minority in most nineteenth-century societies since they were excluded from the political franchise. The problem with the Abrahamic faith is that they are simultaneously universalistic (faith is the basis of membership) and exclusive (there is only one faith): how then could they accept minority status? Modern Christianity has solved the problem through a separation of politics and religion in which conscience is relegated to the private sphere. Judaism, through the creation of a territorial solution to the Gentile problem of 'the Jewish question', has made religion the basis of a secular state. Militant Islam defines 'Household of Islam' as a space within which political and religious identities overlap. The problem is that existing nation-state boundaries do not necessarily correspond to the boundaries of faith.

My argument is that, while popular struggles (through class conflict, warfare and migration) are crucial to the development of citizenship-claims as abatements of exploitation within capitalist society, the historical emergence of citizenship may also owe a great deal to the universalistic thrusts of the Abrahamic faiths. In particular, Christianity and Islam conceive the political in terms of an anti-kinship ideology, so that the Church and the household of faith pave the way to notions of a political community held together by ideology rather than by blood. Islam was a community founded on urban piety rather than on tribal virtue (Turner, 1974a). In the modern world, it is the state through juridic ideology which 'interpellates' the person as an individual citizen. Co-believers have been transformed into co-nationals, but the dilemma of universalism and exclusion remains the same. If Ernest Gellner is correct that language becomes the basis of citizenship and a centralized educational system is the core feature of modern society, modern civility creates subpopulations which are organized and differentiated on the basis of tongues (Gellner, 1964, 1983).

MIGRANTS AND ASSIMILATION

The notion of assimilation as a desirable object of social policy is now widely regarded with suspicion. Assimilation is seen to be political co-optation through acculturation in which minority groups abandon their cultural heritage and identity in the interests of the host community. The assimilation of minorities is thus parallel to the incorporation of the working classes within the dominant culture. It is often thought that migrants are bought off through minor concessions to subcultural practices, work conditions and specific group interests: assimilation is the neutralization of protest. An alternative argument would be that popular struggles have two aspects, being simultaneously radical and non-radical in terms of their implication for the continuity of the status quo. The character of citizenship in specific circumstances would then be an empirical rather than a theoretical/moral issue. Such an answer is ultimately unsatisfactory and in any case the argument developed in this analysis of the roots of democracy has been that citizenship is inherently progressive and radical in representing real changes in society with major implications for traditional forms of exploitation between workers and employers, men and women, children and parents. Where assimilation through the achievement of citizenship rights within the host community is a consequence of collective struggles, assimilation is not inevitably a sell-out of genuine, radical aspirations. By contrast, where assimilation is handed down from above, it involves the acculturation of the individual within the host community without any change in the balance of political power. Such a process of acculturation appears to have been the predominant feature of Jewish assimilation in France around the time of the Dreyfus affair (Marrus, 1971).

The conclusion is that adherence to a subnational culture is typically a defensive mechanism to preserve cultural identities as the basis for waging conflict against a more powerful host community. Subnational identities thus become frozen around traditional practices and beliefs. The reaffirmation of tradition is thus the method of struggle to maintain an existing niche within the society and of mobilizing dissent against the wider host community. Subcultural dissent is thus based upon a backward sloping curve of tradition. Since assimilation is characteristically through intermarriage, the abandonment of the traditional faith and the dilution of language, subculturalism tends to reinforce the control of fathers over daughters, priests over the community and educators over the illiterate; the Celtic fringe in Great Britain, the Jewish Shtetl in Europe and the *dhimmis* of Islam were culturally traditionalist for these reasons of self-defence (Gibb and Bowen, 1957; Brotz, 1964; Gregorovius, 1966;

Neuwirth, 1969; Poll, 1969; Fried, 1982). Hence, subcommunities in societies which are secular, urban and industrial often assume the status of cultural museums. Collective struggles against colonial powers have often had the consequences of modernizing gender, role, family organization and political attitudes, but when struggles for minority status result, not in assimilation but in a further isolation of subgroups in their traditional culture, then the museum-effect is intensified. When conflict over minority status brings about real changes in the market place as a result of usurpational struggles, the defensive attachment to traditional practices is no longer necessary to social existence. Particularistic subnational cultures are then perceived as anarchic and as a barrier to social mobility and improvements in standards of living. At this stage, the argument against assimilation itself becomes, in the literal sense, reactionary. Assimilation may be threatening to traditional holders of power within the subcommunity, because their conservative hold over the family is undermined or at least threatened by the social mobility of the younger generation. It is for this reason that it has been argued that citizenship is essentially incompatible with patriarchy as much as with class domination, and therefore the expansion of citizenship is the primary criterion of social modernization. The paradox is that modernization of the citizen may be incompatible with the capitalist development of the economy, because citizenship requires a redistribution of power within the family and a redistribution of wealth within the society as a whole. The struggle for citizenship as a result largely explains the uneven development of industrial societies in the various routes out of premodern societies.

4
Social Movements

CITIZENSHIP AND PARTICIPATION

In this study, I have defined citizenship, following T. H. Marshall, in terms of social participation, where participation can be defined in terms of three elements, namely civil, political and social participation. Citizenship involves essentially the question of access to scarce resources in society and participation in the distribution and enjoyment of such resources. Whereas political theory typically considers citizenship in terms of civil and political rights of access to decision-making and the selection of government, a broader notion of citizenship involves the question of social membership and participation in society as a whole. The boundaries which define citizenship thus ultimately define membership of a social group or collectivity. In somewhat simple terms, animals are not citizens because they are not social members and they are not social members because they have no legitimate access to rights of a social, political and civil kind. This simple definition of citizenship immediately raises the more complex question of what it is to have social membership. That is, why are animals not social members? Since the boundary between nature and society is problematic and unstable, the ultimate definition of citizenship is itself vague and uncertain. To become a citizen involves a successful definition of the self as a bona fide member of society and thus as a legitimate recipient of social rights. Becoming a citizen involves a process of, as it were, getting into society as an outcome of social struggles. Entry into citizenship thus involves a process of social conflict and negotiation since citizenship is defined by various forms of social closure which exclude outsiders and preserve the rights of insiders to the full enjoyment of welfare and other social benefits. An expansion of citizenship involves some form of struggle where through a usurpational strategy a group of outsiders successfully gains entry into the area of society in order to make claims on scarce resources (Parkin, 1979).

The classical debate in sociology over the nature of citizenship in relationship to capitalism has been dominated by the question of social class, so that the struggles for citizenship have been seen in terms of class conflict. Thus, in the debate which followed T. H. Marshall's definition of citizenship and its function in capitalist society, the history of citizenship in British society was seen in terms of the history of the English working classes to gain political and social rights within contemporary capitalism. The history of the nineteenth century was essentially the history of the struggles of the working classes through trade unionism and political parties to gain a political franchise and to expand the rights of their class to social security and social welfare. A number of classical studies in social history, especially by Marxist historians, documented the conflicts of the working classes against the owners of property, the formation of working-class militant groups and the eventual success of the working classes in establishing unions and achieving political rights (Hobsbawm, 1959, 1964; Thompson, 1963; Hobsbawm and Rudé, 1969). By comparison with the working classes in other European societies in the nineteenth century, the British working classes were relatively successful in achieving unionization and political rights. The British Reform Acts of 1832, 1867, 1884 and 1918 had the consequence of expanding the political franchise to incorporate first the middle classes and then the working classes into British political life. Legislation on health, education and safety at work can also be seen as part of an extension of social citizenship to these classes. While the working classes on the Continent were radical and revolutionary in their political aspirations, the British working classes have been seen as reformist and incorporated rather than revolutionary classes (Lichtheim, 1970). Although the British working classes were politically active in seeking representation within society and participation in the democratic process, the end of political participation was achieved only 'because it was obvious to all that the articulate section of the working class had abandoned its revolutionary aspirations and could safely be trusted with the vote' (Cole and Postgate, 1961,

p. 390). The assimilation of the working classes into the capitalist system has been seen as a consequence of: the predominance of religious perspectives among the working classes (Thompson, 1963): the early destruction of the Chartist movement before the development of a revolutionary, working-class ideology (Anderson, 1964); the spread of individualism in the working classes via the labour aristocracy (Cousins and Davis, 1974); and finally the bribery of the working classes by capitalists as an outcome of the wealth produced by imperialism (Lenin, 1965).

In the twentieth century, sociologists and social historians commenting on the political role of the working classes in Britain have continued to argue that the working classes are largely assimilated into capitalism as a consequence of citizenship which is seen to be a form of sham democracy. Arguments which were first elaborated in the nineteenth century have been supplemented by a range of new theories which suggest that twentieth-century incorporation of the working classes is also brought about by new processes such as embourgeoisement. The postwar period of affluence created a new set of working-class attitudes towards capitalism, which encouraged pragmatic acceptance of capitalist conditions in a period of rising real wages. The affluent worker was privatized and did not develop any community solidarity with the working classes. Their attitude to work was instrumentalist in the sense that it was merely a means to individual consumption. With the decline of traditional heavy industry, there has been a corresponding erosion of the traditional working classes and a decline of the working-class electorate. The working classes were also fragmented by loyalties which divided along ethnic, regional and gender dimensions. It was argued by sociologists in the 1970s that these were not the conditions which historically had given rise to a radical social consciousness, geared to the need for fundamental structural changes in the fabric of capitalist society (Bottomore, 1971). In this same period in Great Britain the Labour party ceased to offer any effective opposition to Tory monetarism, with the Labour vote declining from 14 million in 1951 to 11 million in 1979 when the electorate had actually increased by 5 million new voters.

In the debate over social participation in capitalism, social class is often opposed to citizenship in the sense that it is normally argued that it is impossible to achieve full and real participation in a society which is fundamentally unequal in terms of class divisions. Although the argument has been pursued in terms of this dichotomy of citizenship and class, it should be noted that 'class' represents a major problem in both the Marxist and sociological approaches to the nature of social stratification in contemporary capitalism. The validity of Marxist class analysis has been much disputed in recent years (Giddens, 1973; Abercrombie and Urry, 1983; Cottrell, 1984).

It is unlikely that Marxism as a social theory could ever abandon the concept of class and remain coherent as a perspective on modern societies but Marxism generally has failed to answer the analytical problems raised by sociological theory and research with respect to the character of class structures in modern societies. These are too well known to rehearse here but the basic issues are concerned with the definitions and dimensions of classes, the emergence of new classes and the ambiguous location of middle classes, the decline of classes and the reformation of the class structure in late capitalism, and finally the nature of class consciousness and class imagery (Giddens and Held, 1982). Another problem which is central to the discussion of the nature of citizenship is that class analysis has proved notoriously inadequate as a framework for the study of gender relationships, ethnic relationships and gerontology. That is, class analysis has normally taken a reductive stance towards such apparently nonclass factors as sex, age and cultural differences. Many dimensions of the struggle for social participation have little or nothing to do directly with social class relationships, but involve the protest movements of minority groups to achieve greater participation within the social and legal structure of a society. The debate about citizenship, at least in the English context, has largely neglected a range of issues which are crucial in white colonial-settler societies, in North America and in societies where caste is an important dimension of social stratification. Apart from certain American exceptions, the debate about citizenship within the British context has been excessively narrow in its approach. The post-Marshall debate has not extended the analysis of citizenship outside the context of class to take into consideration feminism, debates about the rights of children and issues relating to the moral status of animals and nature.

The problem of class analysis in contemporary Marxism has many theoretical and empirical roots but one important modern consideration was the attempt to understand the 1968 crisis in French society where most of the conventional forms of analysis seemed inadequate to an understanding of the new social movements which were transforming French culture and society. It is now obvious that much of the conflict and political change of modern society is located in a number of diverse social movements which have a complex class composition but which clearly extend well beyond a class basis. In attempting to come to terms theoretically with these phenomena, a number of Marxist and radical sociologists have turned to the concept of 'social movement'.

The analysis of social movements owes a considerable debt to social anthropology which concerned itself with so-called nativistic or revitalization movements when anthropologists became concerned to understand the development of, for example, cargo cults in the struggle for colonial independence in the postwar period. The debate about 'collective behaviour' became a marked feature of functionalist sociology in the early 1960s when the analysis of social movements was an important feature of the sociological inquiry into social change in social systems (Turner and Killian, 1957; Smelser, 1962; Wilkinson, 1971). The notion of social movements was subsequently adopted by French Marxist and radical sociology to analyse the social movements which had so massively disrupted French life in the late 1960s (Castells, 1977, 1978; Touraine, 1984).

While the notion of social movements has been much criticized, I wish to suggest that the notion of social movement is important in understanding the nature of the drive for citizenship participation by groups and collectivities which cannot be analysed exclusively by their class composition. That is, the notion of social movement provides us with a valid approach when understanding the expanding nature of citizenship claims within recent capitalist history. The objections to it can be stated briefly. It is difficult to isolate the essential elements which constitute a social movement and hence a great variety of social phenomena can be categorized in this way. For example, collective behaviour has been defined as 'mobilization on the basis of a belief which re-defines social action' (Smelser, 1962, p. 8). Such a definition embraces cargo cults, political movements, trade-union movements and urban social movements from a variety of societies under a diversity of conditions. Other authors have suggested that the notion of social movements refers to historically specific attempts in the modern period by self-conscious organizations to bring about social change in order to remedy strains in the social system (Banks, 1972). Another difficulty with the concept is that social movements vary considerably in their degree of internal organization, hierarchical structure and developed ideology so that it is difficult to know whether a crowd is a social movement in the same way that British trade unionism was a social movement in the nineteenth century (Rudé, 1959).

There are times when the search for terminological purity is less than rewarding if not unnecessary and prohibitive. The majority of sociological concepts is typically contested and problematic, referring to diverse and contradictory phenomena so that the attempt to achieve conceptual clarity may have the effect of diminishing the richness of a sociological approach. The concepts of 'alienation' and 'anomie' are two well-known examples, where the search for terminological precision and conceptual clarity has not been achieved but the concepts have nevertheless proved immensely valuable in sociological research (Lukes, 1967). Definitions of social movements, regardless of the theoretical perspective within which they are located, typically refer to a cluster of factors as the essential elements of a social movement and this set of factors normally includes some reference to the idea of collective action in order to change or defend a feature of the society, where these actions are combined with an overt ideology and self-consciousness of purpose in an organization with a high degree of flexibility and an absence of a specific locale (Giddens, 1984, p. 204). For the purpose of this argument the definition offered by Tom Bottomore will suffice, namely that a social movement involves 'collective endeavour to promote or resist change in the society of which it forms part' (Bottomore, 1979, p. 41).

The complexity of the definition of social movement is to some extent a reflection of the complexity of social movements themselves in the context of modern politics. It also reflects the fact that the conceptual framework of traditional sociology with its emphasis on class relationships has both neglected social movements and also failed to provide an adequate place for social movements in mainstream sociology. Contemporary social movements have the following important characteristics. They recruit from a wide diversity of social classes and social groups; in particular, they are characterized by fluctuating alliances between intellectuals, the middle classes (especially in public service) and minority groups (especially ethnic and cultural minorities). Their organization is characterized by extreme flexibility and often a studied absence of formal lines of communication. Social movements tend therefore to have localized leadership and localized membership where this membership is drawn together periodically in what might be termed episodic socio-dramas which have the effect of drawing media attention to the political objectives of such groups. The new social movements of the 1970s and 1980s have proved enormously successful in winning television coverage and media interest in their activities. The new social movements also typically adhere to a general social philosophy which embraces a strong interest in environmental politics and conservationism. These movements thus raise in an acute form the whole relationship between nature and society, culture and animality; they have been strongly influenced by the whole question of the domination of nature not only by capitalism but by modern industrial society generally. Because such movements have been concerned with the question of environmental pollution, they have often joined hands with the interests of minority groups, especially aboriginal groups where the aboriginals are seen to be the natural protectors and inheritors of a pure environment. Unlike large-scale industry, aboriginal pastoralism is not a threat to nature or to the continuity of human society, and aboriginal culture is typically seen as having a contribution to make to methods of managing nature which are less intrusive and exploitative than those which characterize capitalist society. Since white-settler colonialism destroyed the aboriginals while also polluting the environment, the restoration of aboriginal rights coincides with attempts to protect the environment from contemporary industrial exploitation (Rowley, 1975). The critique of the domination of society has thus been fused with the critique of the domination of nature in modern social movements which combine social, cultural and environmental issues (Leiss, 1972). As a result the new social movements tend to be umbrella organizations for a diversity of complex interests and political issues in which questions of exploitation, environmental control and peace are fused within a single campaign (Eyerman, 1982; Keane, 1984).

Social movements which aim to change society in the name of a generalized belief inevitably raise questions about the nature of participation in society and thus are inevitably movements about the rights of citizenship. The growth of citizenship in western industrial societies can be seen as the outcome, intended or unintended, of a diversity of social movement over the last two centuries. Citizenship rights are the outcome of social movements which aim either to expand or to defend the definition of social membership and the long-term consequence of such social movements has been to elaborate and universalize the notion of citizenship to embrace a wider group of 'persons' and the expansion of the notion of personhood has in contemporary society begun to incorporate the notion of 'nature'. The existing debate about citizenship therefore as a relationship between class and social membership is too narrow to deal with the new issues of citizenship which raise legal problems concerning the political status of children, embryos, invertebrate species and inanimate forms of nature.

FROM PARTICULAR TO UNIVERSAL CITIZENS

We can conceptualize the development of citizenship as a series of circles or waves which expand outwards from a narrow and particular definition of the citizen where these waves eventually embrace human and nonhuman 'personalities'. In the early stages of English capitalism the citizen was essentially the male property-holding head of the household, and real political power and real citizenship was held in the hands of a narrow cross-section of society. The first rights of citizenship were possessive in the sense that social participation and power were restricted to those who were owners of property (Macpherson, 1962). The paradox in Locke's theory of political rights was the conflict between the notion of majority rule and rule by property owners. How could the rights of property be defended in a society where majority rule provided the basis for political authority? This contradiction was of course the abiding problem of liberal democracy which both espoused the criterion of universal egalitarianism and the principle of enlightened and educated decision-making by a select elite which had a commitment to the continuity of society. The problem for the liberal elite was the question of the illiberal majority which might overthrow the very principles of individual decision-making. This problem can be seen constantly repeated in the work of de Tocqueville, J. S. Mill, Rousseau and Spencer (Wolin, 1961). The English liberal tradition as represented by J. S. Mill feared that rule by the majority would bring about a stultifying conformity which would so restrict individual conscience as to undermine eventually culture and society. In practice the threat of mass society meant the threat of the working classes to dominate parliamentary politics in a way which would undermine the authority and control of the enlightened middle-class utilitarians. The result of these anxieties was to restrict effective citizenship to a particularistic criterion – namely, the legitimate ownership of property – and we can see the struggle for social participation as an attempt by organized, working-class groups to expand this definition of citizenship to embrace the working classes alongside other social classes within the political system. This struggle by the working classes to achieve civil and political rights should be seen alongside other transformations of the nature of personality and citizenship in the late eighteenth and nineteenth centuries whereby the status of children and slaves became involved with a debate about political rights generally (Davis, 1970). This expansion of political rights also corresponded to an increase in the social protection of children and women by the Factory Acts and this development of social rights was bound up fundamentally with the whole emergence of the child as a distinctive and separate category of person who required protection within the public sphere (Ariés, 1973; Grylls, 1978).

One index of this transformation and expansion of social participation can be located in certain important changes in the character of art in the nineteenth century, especially in the French tradition. My argument is that what counts as a suitable topic for artwork is a strong indication of what societies consider to be valuable and thus changes in the content of representational art may be used as a measure of the nature of citizenship or at least the distribution of power in societies. There were important changes in French art in the nineteenth century in terms of technique, audience and patronage which reflect the changing status of 'the common man'. The growth of so-called Realism is an important measure of the increasing significance of the world and life of ordinary citizens in French society. Art in the Middle Ages had been essentially religious art under the patronage of the Church but it had also reflected the dominance of the land-owning feudal class. The dominance of the Church and the feudal land-owning class was reflected in the dominance of pictorial representations of religious themes on the one hand and paintings of kings and queens on the other. El Greco's painting 'The Burial of Count Orgaz' with its strong representation of a hierarchical, social and spiritual order descending from Christ to his bishops and the aristocracy is a good illustration of art depicting the privileged structure of a world with limited citizenship. This aristocratic representation of death should be contrasted with Gustave Courbet's 'A Burial at Ornans' which depicts a mundane burial in a naturalistic environment where 'ordinary people' are gathered round a burial site where the dominant themes are secular (Nochlin, 1971). The French peasantry and working classes became the primary topic of realist painting and the realist style was naturalistic, secular, positivist and mundane. Realistic art like science was seen to be a radical and secular commentary which was in many respects descriptive rather than prescriptive. The realists in France and the pre-Raphaelite brotherhood in England came to celebrate the significance of work and the dignity of labour as appropriate topics for art; Madox Brown's 'Work' is probably the most famous representation of this new interest in the world of work and labour. The realist tradition was closely associated with political radicalism, with the emergence of the working classes and the decline of traditional structures and values in European society. The development of realist art can be seen therefore as a cultural index of the growing significance of the working classes in cultural and political life as an effect of social struggles and social movements for the enhancement of rights of citizenship.

The development of the working classes and the achievement of political enfranchisement created certain moral and political anomalies, since it left women completely outside the realm of politics and public life. The expansion of citizenship to men and the decline of property as the sole criterion of social participation left women in an anomalous social and political position. The feminist movement and in particular the Suffragette Movement can be seen as political attempts by organized women to gain egalitarian political and social rights which had been successfully won by male members of the working classes. Women who were involved in the struggle to achieve political rights for the working classes had been radicalized politically and the absence of rights for women were seen to be incompatible with democratic principles. The struggle for universalistic criteria of social participation has an internal logic whereby particularistic exclusions from social participation are seen to be increasingly incompatible with rational principles of political discourse. Women could use rights achieved by men to promote their own cause regardless of the interests and beliefs of men. There seems to be a general principle that ideological conflicts can provide the model for excluded groups to achieve social membership. The middle classes use individualism as an attack on aristocratic principles and subsequently the working classes often mobilized bourgeois individualism to attack the middle classes on the grounds of inconsistency.

It can be reasonably argued that the growth of citizenship rights for women was a consequence of wartime conditions and female employment in heavy industry rather than an enlightened altruism on the part of political parties which explains the development of legislation. It could also be suggested that the transformation of women's status in society is an effect of the changing structure of the household as a consequence of transformations in the nature of property ownership in late capitalism (Turner, 1983). In addition there were important changes in family culture in relationship to the concept of romantic love and the care of children which did much to change the public status of women. These changes were also associated with shifts in the nature of female employment and the development of contraceptive devices which gave women greater control over both their public and private lives (Shorter, 1977, 1982).

Some feminist writers often suggest that these changes in the political and social status of women were relatively superficial in that the real nature of the sexual division of labour in society was left unchallenged and untouched by these legal or formal changes (Barrett and McIntosh, 1982). This argument appears difficult to sustain. The effect of the Matrimonial Causes Acts of the nineteenth century and other changes in divorce procedures in the twentieth century have had the consequence of not only equalizing the relationship between men and women in marriage, but constituting women as legal personalities. Before this legislation, women literally lost their legal status on marriage since their legal personalities were submerged in that of their husbands. Although women are discriminated against in employment and in social rights, there exists legislation whereby women can mount claims to equal treatment and there has been some change in the nature of recruitment of women to full-time occupations including the professions. Although there is much evidence that women are still excluded from the higher echelons of the professions, there is also evidence of a general improvement in the recruitment of women to law, medicine and the paramedical occupations (Kobrin, 1966; Epstein, 1970; Murgatroyd, 1982; Marshall, 1984). My argument is not that legal changes in women's citizenship rights have resulted in empirical changes in the equality of men and women such as to eradicate sexual prejudice against women. On the contrary, there is clear evidence that women competing on the market with men are discriminated against despite the existence of formal legislation and changing attitudes towards women. However, it is the case that there have been major improvements in the status of women as a consequence of the women's social movement and not simply as an outcome of functional requirements of capitalism. To take one example it is impossible to read Elizabeth Blackwell's *Opening the Medical Profession to Women* (1977), which was originally published in 1895, without being convinced of the reality of the massive changes in the status of women in the medical profession and related paramedical professions over the past eighty years. It would be equally difficult to read a biography of Florence Nightingale (see Woodham-Smith, 1950) without being convinced that the status of nurses in society has also been radically changed as a consequence of political action by nurses and as a consequence of changing attitudes towards women in society generally. While some feminist writers wish to describe the nurse/doctor/patient relationship as patriarchal (Gamarnikow, 1978) a longer historical consideration of the status and outlook of nurses suggests that there has been a transformation of nurses' attitudes towards doctors so that the compliance of female nurses to male doctors is no longer guaranteed by the hierarchical structure of the hospital (Hughes, Hughes and Deutscher, 1958). These discriminatory relationships between men and women in the workplace and in the domestic sphere are best described as patristic rather than patriarchal – that is, they involve open conflict and struggle between groups in a context where the formal and legal structure of patriarchalism has largely collapsed (Turner, 1984b).

The first wave of citizenship had the consequence of demoting the formal role of property in the definition of citizen. The second wave of citizenship from the women's movement had the consequence of demoting gender as the definition of citizenship. As a consequence of the women's movement, the third wave of citizenship involved a redefinition of age and kinship ties within the family as a significant feature of the legal definition of citizenship rights. If gender could not be regarded as an appropriate feature of exclusion from society, the status of children and the aged also became increasingly insignificant in defining membership within society. Social legislation on children and the rights of the elderly can be regarded as a social provision for citizenship claims irrespective of age, character of dependency or position within the kinship group. Of course, in earlier societies when kinship was defined by property it was empirically the case that heads of households, in addition to enjoying patriarchal authority, enjoyed gerontocracy as a basis of their power. Thus, in early colonial America, age was an important criterion of power and authority. With the ageing of the population and a distinctive shift in values towards youth, the aged have been marginalized and victimized in society with the consequence that their control over the resources of citizenship has been diminished (Johnson and Williamson, 1980). Age as a criterion of social membership, however, becomes increasingly anomalous since age is an ascriptive category and ascriptive categories are difficult to reconcile with a universalistic norm of citizenship. Decisions about an appropriate age of consent, appropriate age groups for education, military service and social involvement, and legal norms giving protection to dependants become increasingly arbitrary in a context where age appears to be particularistic and ascribed. In particular, making distinctions between the rights of children and the rights of parents where children have ceased to be the legal property of their parents becomes a complex and conflictual area of law relating to civil liberties (Tutt, 1984). These anomalies in civil status are an indication of the expanding nature of claims on citizenship whereby property, gender and age are no longer appropriate in defining social membership.

The fourth wave of expanding citizenship rights is brought about by social movements which in fact have the consequence of ascribing rights to nature and the environment. Social movements to protect nature from human exploitation are attributing rights to animals and organic phenomena in the same way that social movements in the nineteenth century ascribed rights to women and to the working classes. These movements also illustrate an important point, especially in Marxist sociology, that the man–society–nature relationship is essentially historical and variable. One consequence of the transformative capacity of human labour is that, as Marx noted in his commentary on needs, the natural boundaries of society are constantly pushed backwards as a consequence of the social advance of human potentialities. The limits of the natural environment are reduced by the very development of these social capacities as nature becomes 'the inorganic body' of man (Marx, 1967, p. 293). In his ontology Marx was concerned to understand the relationship between 'the naturalization of man' and the 'humanization of nature'. Marx understood this relationship in terms of the historical development of collective labour whereby, as a result of transforming nature by their labour, human beings came also to transform themselves by their appropriation of nature. It was in this sense that Marx felt that the development of human societies involved a constant transformation of the nature–society relationship as human labour came constantly to appropriate and constitute nature in the service of these collective interests. Nature becomes the site of human potentiality and, while nature is an alien force, it is constantly appropriated and possessed as a consequence of human activity, in particular by human sensuous practice. Nature which is a thing-in-itself becomes as a consequence of these historical practices a thing-for-man. While nature exists as an external reality it is also transformed and socially appropriated, becoming part of the internal structure of human development.

We can apprehend the growth of citizenship historically as a diminution of these natural boundaries separating people from nature. Social participation can be seen as a transition from an external natural condition to an internal social condition within the social system. For example, it has often been argued that the subordinate position of women in history is a function of their association with nature such that only men are the producers of human culture (Ortner, 1974), but the political enfranchisement of women in competitive capitalism begins to undermine and break the ancient, patriarchal connection between the state, the household and the dominance of husbands. In modern capitalism, this barrier of nature is rolled back even further in so far as animals and inorganic matter begin to acquire legal status and political rights with a minimum of protection from scientific experimentation and exploitation. The development of animals into a quasi-citizenship position can be dated in the British context from Martins Act of 1822 which proscribed cruelty to large domesticated animals such as horses and cows, and the Cruelty to Animals Act of 1877 which began to control experimentation on living vertebrate animals. The antivivisectionist movement and the work of the RSPCA can also be regarded as a social lobby in favour of the inclusion of vertebrates within the sphere of social citizenship (French, 1975).

The legal status of animals is in most contemporary industrial societies quite anomalous. We might suggest that one indicator of the legal status of an animal resides in the question of whether it can be eaten. Within the diet of most families, we could say that cod and chickens have relatively low legal status and are obviously excluded from the notion of citizenship. However, dogs which are domesticated pets are normally protected under law from being consumed by their owners. The status of a dairy cow which is owned on a small farm and approaches the status of a domesticated pet is peculiar in the sense that there is no legal prohibition on consuming such a beast. The contrast between the status of the cow and the dog in western cultures is an interesting illustration of the relativity of legal and social rights. The contrast is obvious when one considers that the cow has a sacred status in Hindu societies whereas for the Chinese the dog is an important aspect of cuisine. The question is: are dogs citizens in the making? The character of such legal personalities on the margins of society illustrates the contention of my argument that citizenship expands outwards creating anomalies on the periphery of society which are typically resolved by law in a universalistic manner. Citizenship expands in such a way as to undermine anomalies and to resolve questions of citizenship in favour of universalistic and achieved categories rather than ascribed status positions.

GOD AND HIS CITIZENS

If Marxist sociology is correct in arguing that the image of God in any society is the representation of the alienated potentialities of people, then the history of the conceptualization of God should provide us with a strong index of the development of the notion of citizenship (Turner, 1983). The argument of this chapter is that, as a consequence of the conflict between social movements, there is a tendency for citizenship to become more abstract and universal. Therefore, a consideration of the relationship between man, God and society should provide us with a measure of this growing universality. Such a picture of the history of religion is implicit in much sociology of religion especially in the work of Fustel de Coulanges who in *The Ancient City* described the growing abstraction of classical religion as a consequence of the transformation of the political structure of imperial Rome

(Turner, 1971). Thus theological conceptions of spiritual space in terms of a set of hierarchical relationships between God, angels, man and animals can be interpreted as also reflections upon the dominant hierarchical structures of secular space. Marxist theories of religion have similarly seen the theological problems of any age as an outcome of the class relationships of a given society, so that the central problems of class relationships tend to find their reflection in the central problems of the theological paradigm. The notion of the 'tragic vision' in the theology of Pascal, for example, can be connected with the problem of a declining social class in the French social structure (Goldmann, 1964). Briefly, the status of spiritual citizens within the kingdom of God can be taken as a social index of the social status of citizens within the human polity.

We can thus provide a sketch in Christendom of the changing God–human relationship from feudalism to capitalism in terms of a declining hierarchical relationship and the emergence of a universalistic conceptualization of God as an abstract personality. In the Judeo-Christian tradition the impact of Jewish nomadic pastoral conditions was to be seen in the conceptualization of God as The Good Shepherd and the patriarch but under feudal conditions the social structure of heaven is reproduced in terms of the hierarchical structure of feudal strata. The hierarchical gradation of Dante's world was perfectly reproduced in the fourteenth century *Commedia* with its fine distinctions of virtue and worth. The Protestant Reformation challenged and transformed these hierarchical structures and, while leaving the state as a crucial feature of secular authority, brought about a certain individualization of the person in relationship to deity. Max Weber's account of this relationship in Calvinism in *The Protestant Ethic and the Spirit of Capitalism* has become one of the hall-marks of sociological interpretation of these transformed conceptions. God could no longer be controlled or influenced by magic, sacraments or by ecclesiastical authority. For example, John Milton's *Paradise Lost* stands at the conjuncture of the old forces of feudal ranking and the new world of individualized man, since his conceptualization of heaven is largely feudal with Christ, the archangels, angels, the heavenly host and the world of men as the principal orders, but his view of individual powers is summarized paradoxically in the person of Satan. The evolution of theological thought with respect to this relationship can be well illustrated by the emergence in the eighteenth century of a conception of human responsibility in terms of the stewardship of talents which implies a new conception of social accountancy whereby human debits and credits are balanced at the end of life. God has been transformed from the good shepherd to the feudal lord to the ultimate accountant.

The imagery of God was nevertheless perceived through patriarchal secular structures, since God by definition had to be an old householder and it is interesting that in colonial America with gerontocracy as the principal social authority that God had to be an elderly patriarch. However, with the growing democratization of society and the emergence of youth as a special value the notion and conception of God also changed to become more youthful and more egalitarian. Pre-Raphaelite depictions of God and Christ tended to be romantic but also brought out the human, secular and youthful features of divine powers. This democratization of the image of God probably reached its ultimate level in the USA with the comment by Jane Russell that God was 'a livin' doll' which brought out God's immediacy, intimacy and equality. Such an expression could be regarded as the end product of a feature of Protestantism which Marx and Engels had noted – namely, the relationship between deism and abstract commodity relationships. More importantly, the egalitarian view of God corresponds to the emergence of the abstract, juridic citizen as the central point of the modern legal polity. In contemporary society, God becomes more abstract, while also becoming increasingly dehumanized. The traditional anthropomorphic metaphors of spirituality will no longer suffice since they are by definition particularistic. God is stripped of his gender identity while also being robbed of any ethnic or cultural attributes. God is no longer the old white patriarch but a Pure Being whose gender, age and other particular attributes have been stripped away. The growth of an abstract deity thus perfectly matches the growth of abstract citizenship.

THE NEO-HEGELIAN IDEALISM?

Hegel's political philosophy sought to reconcile the inherent dualism between the private individual locked in the particularity of private space and the generality of the citizen inhabiting the public world of politics. Hegel attempted to resolve this dichotomy in the evolution of the *polis* where the state would resolve the particular struggle of interest within civil society. It was the state, therefore, which would resolve the political alienation of the private person in the public life of the *polis*. In short, Hegel conceptualized citizenship in terms of the growing abstraction and universalism of the state. Marx's critique of this political philosophy is well known (Hyppolite, 1969; Kolakowski, 1978, Vol. 1). In capitalism, the state is merely the expression of underlying class conflicts rather than the resolution of the contradictions of civil society. The state is not an abstract judge resolving the problems of capitalist society but, on the contrary, a partisan protector of capitalist interests. The state cannot resolve the contradiction between the private individual and the public citizen, and Hegel's glorification of the Prussian state was thus an apology for particularistic powers. The alienation of the citizen and the division between public and private reality could only be resolved by a revolutionary transformation of capitalist society. In bourgeois capitalism the abstract of rights of the citizen were merely a smoke-screen which mystified the real nature of conflicting interests and the powerlessness of the working classes. The argument here is not teleological and no optimistic or evolutionary assumptions are part of this study.

First, it is assumed that the outcome of the struggles of social movements and subordinate groups is largely unintended, contingent and accidental and that no necessary transformation of any particular status is guaranteed by modern political history. The development of citizenship is not an evolutionary unfolding of the Spirit of some universal essence but rather the consequence of a whole series of particular conflicts between social groups and the development of social movements for rights and civil liberties. The outcome of such struggles may be either the development of citizenship or the erosion of previously established rights. Citizenship has a certain logic since, once it is accepted that rights cannot be particular and ascriptive, it then becomes difficult to exclude women and children on the grounds of gender and age. Furthermore, it is argued that social movements provide models of change for subsequent groups in their struggle for rights and membership of society. For example, the struggle of American protestors against the war in Vietnam provided a model for struggles for civil libertarians and in particular it galvanized American women and formed the basis for subsequent women's movements. In a similar fashion the Tasmanian Wilderness Society adopted the beliefs and strategies of Green Peace movements which had been successful in Europe.

Secondly, it is not assumed that these universalistic norms of citizenship cannot be reversed, undermined, withdrawn or abandoned. Indeed it is assumed that any growth of citizenship provides a challenge to existing patterns of power and authority and therefore any growth of citizenship will be met with political struggles by dominant groups to preserve their advantages within the status quo. This was particularly obvious in the aftermath of the French Revolution when in Germany significant steps were taken to dismantle the Napoleonic reforms. In Germany the policies of Frederick William III were designed to re-establish the old order with the aid of the squirearchy against the interests of both the middle class and workers; it was against this background that Marx developed his whole view of social rights (Berlin, 1978). In France, with the abdication of Napoleon in 1814, there was a restoration of traditional authorities and the creation of a constitutional monarchy which through the nineteenth century placed a significant brake on the aspirations of radical political leaders (Cobban, 1961, Vol. 2). In Great Britain the social rights of citizenship which had been achieved in the 1940s and 1950s have to some extent been undermined by the monetarist economic policies of Conservative governments in the 1970s and 1980s. In this context, the conflict between welfare and market is a perfect illustration of Marshall's elaboration of the notion of hyphenated society in which there is a contradictory relationship between the demand for public utilities and private profitability (Goldthorpe, 1978; Hirst, 1982). Reagonomics and Thatcherism represent the dismemberment of the Keynesian revolution of the 1930s which instituted a public policy of government demand-management to reduce unemployment and stimulate economic growth (Frank, 1982).

Thirdly, it is also assumed that rights will tend to be contradictory and that the growth of rights for one social group may involve a contraction of rights for others. For example, the right of women to control their own bodies has been expressed through a variety of legal developments such as abortion reform. However, women's rights over their own bodies may conflict with the rights of children, especially unborn children (Shorter, 1982). The right of abortion has raised the problematic issue of when a fertilized embryo is a legal person and involves a political decision about the citizenship rights of unborn children. If we assume that a woman has a property right over her own embryos, who has control over transplanted embryos? There are in certain respects contradictory rights and interests between women and children, or at least contradictory claims between natural and social parentage. There are similar contradictions relating to questions of age where the demands of elderly citizens to enjoy rights to employment may conflict with the claims of unemployed youth in an economic context of significant recession and technological de-skilling.

Finally, this study of citizenship has identified different patterns of modernization giving rise to different political cultures and, in particular, has identified a 'deformed route' to contemporary politics in white colonial-settler societies where racism has often been institutionalized through the legal system. Rhodesia and South Africa, while being exposed to patterns of migration, retained through the ideology of Calvinism, a premodern conception of equality and excluded the black communities from political participation. Similarly, while modern Israel had the liberating effect of a migration route to modernity and also possessed an element of secular–socialist doctrine, Israel has arrived at a society which is particularistic in its exclusion of Arabs from real social membership (Rodinson, 1973). The realization of citizenship as an abstract right is thus the consequence of quite specific and concrete social struggles associated with modern social movements to achieve greater participation within society.

5
Individualism and Citizenship

THE INSTITUTIONS OF CITIZENSHIP

The definition of citizenship in classical theory was essentially political. Writers like Jean Bodin regarded citizenship as a status which enjoyed liberty and protection from the state; Thomas Hobbes treated citizenship in terms of the security of one's life under the authority of a state while Locke defined citizenship in terms of security of conscience and property (Walzer, 1970). In Rousseau's political theory the concept of the citizen is very complex and possibly contradictory (Charvet, 1974). In the discussion of the social contract, however, Rousseau defines the citizen as a member of a city which is a corporate and collective body within which the individual personality is submerged; that is, as the product of a political and corporate entity. In a more contemporary context citizenship is often closely associated with nationality and national citizenship is defined simply as membership in a nation-state. One illustration of this approach would be the definition of citizenship as 'official identity' – that is, citizenship involves legal membership in a state (Pranger, 1968). The debate about citizenship leads eventually to an analysis of what constitutes the nation, the state and nationality; thus the question of political citizenship directs us towards an inquiry into the nature of the cultural basis of the contemporary state in language and education (Gellner, 1983).

These conceptualizations of citizenship can be called political because they identify the nature of citizenship with the emergence of political institutions – that is, the classical city and the modern state. To be a citizen is to be a person with political rights involving liberty and protection in return for one's loyalty to the state. The existence of citizenship presupposes a number of political institutions such as the centralized state, a system of political participation, institutions of political education and a variety of institutions associated with the state which protect the individual from the loss of liberties. The central paradox of classical political theory has been to reconcile the claims of the autonomous and free citizen on the one hand with the existence of a centralized and powerful state on the other. The principal explanation which resolves this paradox is the development of a social contract theory whereby the citizen exchanges some aspect of liberty for some aspect of protection. The problem with classical theories of citizenship was the reconciliation of power and freedom by various conceptual devices such as Hobbes' social contract or Rousseau's notion of the general will. Criticisms of political citizenship have typically centred on the impossibility of reconciling individual freedom of conscience with the requirements of public order and stability.

This political conception of citizenship has been attacked by Marxist theories on the grounds that democracy can only be an illusion in capitalist society since the inequality of property rules out any real equality of power. Political citizenship as a theory has also been attacked by conservative theorists such as Michels and Weber on the grounds that mass democracy must entail bureaucracy and bureaucracy must lead to elitism. Mass democracy is subject to 'an iron law of oligarchy' which rules out significant and real participation (Plamenatz, 1973). For Weber, the problem of modern politics is to achieve effective and powerful leadership in a context where bureaucracy and the absence of political consciousness undermine the national political community in a situation where external political and economic forces were very powerful (Eden, 1983). These criticisms suggest that real democracy and genuine citizenship are a sham in contemporary societies because the very institutions which are necessary for citizenship make citizenship impossible. Citizenship can only exist within a nation-state but state power constantly undermines the principle of individual conscience and freedom as a necessary feature of the effective citizen. At least part of the critique of citizenship in this political form rests on a nostalgic view of the Greek *polis* where direct participation was assumed to be real and valid. With the growth of large-scale political institutions, this Greek form of direct participation was no longer possible and citizenship was exposed to the critique of both left and right theoreticians.

It is against the background of this political tradition that we can appreciate the value of T. H. Marshall's approach to citizenship under the three dimensions of civil, political and social rights. Marshall recognized that the civil element of citizenship required certain specific institutions to guarantee individual freedom, such as the liberty of person and the freedom of speech. Under the political element of citizenship he included the rights to participate in the political process and recognized that political citizenship required a number of corresponding institutions such as parliament and local government. However, he introduced the discussion of a social element in citizenship because he realized that civil and political citizenship was incomplete without the rights of economic and social welfare. Corresponding to social citizenship, we find the essential institutions of the educational system and the social services. He went on to argue that the development of social rights of citizenship belongs essentially to the twentieth century with the emergence of the welfare state and contemporary social legislation (Marshall, 1975, 1977). The core of social citizenship is the right to welfare and this right presupposes the existence of a variety of institutions, in particular the existence of a bureaucracy which can deliver these rights on an egalitarian basis, a taxation system whereby the state can acquire the financial means to deliver social welfare, the continuity of a free economic market as the main mechanism for the production of wealth and the existence of a variety of educational institutions to provide a basic and egalitarian system of education (Marshall, 1981). The critique of the political definition of citizenship focused on the incompatibility between personal freedom and the role of the coercive state; the critique of the socioeconomic definition of citizenship is either that citizenship is impossible in capitalism given the continuity of class inequalities or that socioeconomic citizenship requires equality and is thus incompatible with individualism, since equality breeds bureaucracy and bureaucracy destroys individuality. The critique of inequality in modern society is well known in sociology (Brym, 1980). It is important, however, to turn to the liberal and conservative critique of citizenship as bureaucratic equality to understand the problem of individualism in relationship to the growth of socioeconomic rights of modern citizenship.

CITIZENSHIP VERSUS INDIVIDUALISM

If we regard democracy as the essential political environment for the growth of civil and political citizenship, the development of political equality is a necessary feature of the modernization of the state and the political process; citizenship pushes society towards an egalitarian political framework. If we regard the welfare state as a necessary framework for the growth of socioeconomic rights of citizenship, the development of citizenship is associated with an argument in favour of socioeconomic equality. Social citizenship requires a certain level of bureaucracy and state intervention to uphold rights of equality against the tendency of the market to create economic inequality. The various dimensions of citizenship give rise to the principle of equality and equality is often regarded as incompatible with another important value of modern society – namely, individualism. The paradox is that, while citizens are required to be individuals in order to exercise conscience and choice, the institutions which make citizenship possible promote equality and bureaucracy. It appears that citizenship must necessarily breed the social and political conditions which undermine it.

This problem in citizenship and the notion that egalitarian democracy is inimicable to individualism can be traced back in liberal theory and received its classic expression in the work of J. S. Mill in the nineteenth century. Mill's anxieties about the consequences of popular democracy and the adherence to the principle of equality of condition were heightened in the 1840s by his reading of de Tocqueville's book on democracy in America which Mill reviewed in the *Edinburgh Review* in 1840. Although Mill had some critical observations to make on de Tocqueville's argument he was generally sympathetic to the proposition that democracy could bring about a tyranny of the majority over the individual conscience of the citizen. Democratic processes encourage the growth of uniformity of belief and sentiment which were deadening to the idea of individuality which was crucial to Mill's whole outlook (Mill, 1976). Mill believed that the development of reformist politics in Great Britain and the growth of the political franchise would bring about a uniformity of belief which he compared to the uniformity of Chinese despotism, arguing that this dominance of uneducated opinion would bring about a form of Chinese stationariness in British society (Turner, 1974b). Since Mill placed a great emphasis on individuality and saw individual taste as the outcome of appropriate education, it is often difficult to reconcile Mill's individualism with his sense of the importance of a moral community in society. Mill tended to assume fairly contradictory positions towards the role of the community in relationship to self-interest; on occasions he welcomed socialist principles since he felt that communal ownership would compel lazy citizens to contribute to the social whole (Wolin, 1961). These contradictions in liberalism tended to become inflated towards the end of the nineteenth century with the increasing intervention of the state. Thus, in the political philosophy of Herbert Spencer, we see the final liberal attempt to combine individualism with the growth of the state (Peel, 1971). The growth of citizenship as an expansion of socioeconomic rights involved the expansion of the state in the regulation of the market and this conflicted with a favourite liberal principle of the economy – namely, the principle of *laissez-faire*. The increasing role of the state in the organization of education and culture impinged upon the liberal idea of self-education, conscience and self-development in the idea of individuality. The increasing involvement of the ordinary people in the regulation of politics through parliament interfered with the principle of responsible government and leadership by an educated minority. While liberal thought was to some extent dominant in the nineteenth century, there was a crisis in liberal ideology which 'maximised the splendour of freedom of contract – by which, in grim truth, it meant absence of any effective check on capitalist enterprise – and refused, in any profound or coherent way, to consider the state as a potential source of social good' (Laski, 1962, p. 166). The liberal crisis was intensified as a consequence of the gradual decline of the British economy in the second half of the nineteenth century, a decline which undermined the possibility of social welfare in competitive capitalism. Classical liberal economics had no real solution to the economic problems of British capitalism towards the end of the nineteenth century and liberal politics could take no effective measures to counteract the decline or to provide a reasonable social policy for the majority of citizens.

While critics of political citizenship have been concerned with the consequences of mass democracy, there is another strand to the conservative response to growing citizenship which has attacked the idea of economic equality as the central feature of contemporary socioeconomic rights. Equality like citizenship in many respects is a fundamentally modern idea which in its contemporary form dates from the French Revolution with its slogan of liberty, equality and fraternity. In premodern societies, inequality was taken to be the natural condition of people where inequality was typically justified on religious and customary grounds. The inequality of people was either a consequence of previous incarnation or an effect of their essential immorality in a world where men were fallen creatures. There was thus a natural hierarchy of orders: a great chain of being linking God to the lowest of creatures in a natural system of inequality (Lovejoy, 1938). The idea of natural inequality has been challenged as a consequence of revolutionary politics and to some extent has been replaced by the idea that inequality is essentially social rather than natural; inequality is difference plus evaluation (Béteille, 1983). There is a tendency in contemporary social thought to assume that it is inequality rather than equality which requires moral justification, but the problem is that sociological theory generally has asserted that all known human societies are fundamentally unequal regardless of whether they are dominated by the market or by state planning. There appears to be a hiatus between the moral or social commitment to equality as a feature of citizenship and the empirical facts of inequality in human society. It is this hiatus which provides one aspect of the critique of citizenship as equality by both liberal and conservative critics who assume that equality is not feasible as a policy objective of contemporary societies.

AGAINST EQUALITY

In the Marxist tradition the inequalities between individuals are an outcome of the mode of production. Individuals are unequal as a consequence of socioeconomic arrangements and the ultimate root of human inequality is the character of the control over the means of production in society. Classical Marxism argued that these inequalities could be eradicated with a revolutionary transformation of the ownership of the means of production and a redistribution of political power in society with the withering away of state power. For Marxists, inequality is essentially social and historical; it is eradicable by violent political action under appropriate social and economic circumstances. The egalitarian principle of modern citizenship can be satisfied only in a socialist society where the inequality of ownership and distribution has been removed.

Sociologists in the Weberian tradition have been much less sanguine about the possibility of real equality. They have regarded individual inequalities as consequences of market forces (that is, of distribution rather than production) and they have characteristically divided the elements of social stratification into class, status and party. In capitalism inequality can take the form of differences in class positions, in prestige and in political power. Under socialism it is argued that, while inequalities of class can be removed, there is a continuation of inequality of status and power; indeed the inequality of power may be increased in command economies. Party membership becomes the main criterion for advancement within the state bureaucracy (Konrad and Szelenyi, 1979). In centralized socialism there is not only a continuation of power inequalities but, since political and economic power is not differentiated, there is an enhancement of centralized control over the individual and a greater requirement for normative commitment to the system.

Finally, the approach of sociological functionalism which is associated in particular with the work of Kingsley Davis and Wilbert E. Moore sees social stratification as inevitable but also functionally useful for the survival of social systems (Tumin, 1970). In this perspective the hierarchical ordering of positions in society corresponds to the functional importance of various occupations to the continuity and effectiveness of the social system (Davis and Moore, 1945). The competitive market place thus encourages innovation and enterprise which has the effect of producing a system of stratification which more or less corresponds to merit and prestige within a given society. Social inequality ensures that the most significant or important positions in a society are competently and conscientiously occupied by persons who are the most qualified and competent for those tasks. The highest ranking positions in society are those which have the greatest importance for the continuity of society and also require the greatest training and skill. Functionalist theories have seen social stratification as universal in human society, functionally important for society and thus implicitly desirable as a feature of the social structure. Inequality in capitalism and socialism are simply consequences of different organizations of political and economic structures.

While there is massive disagreement amongst sociologists about the explanation of social stratification and also considerable disagreement about what constitutes social stratification, there is relatively little disagreement about the prevalence of stratification and the persistence of inequality. It is useful to distinguish three forms of equality. The first is the ideal of personal equality which argues that human beings qua human beings are necessarily equal. We could suitably call this the principle of ontological equality which asserts an essential equality of people regardless of their historical or social circumstances. It is difficult to separate this principle of equality from some religious, moral or metaphysical tradition which would ground the equality of individuals in some notion of the fatherhood of God. In modern philosophy the ontological notion of equality is ultimately grounded in the tradition which stems from Kant in the categorical imperative that we treat moral persons as ends rather than means. The second type of equality is the equality of opportunity which was expressed in the French Revolution as meaning the career open to the talents. Equality in this sense means equality of access to the means of personal achievement and satisfaction through education and employment. In contemporary social theory this has given rise to the notion of a society based upon meritocracy which would be a modern version of the Chinese bureaucracy based upon a ladder of success (Ho, 1964).

Finally there is the notion of an equality of outcomes or of result which is the most radical notion of equality. According to this principle, equality should be independent of achievement, merit or other particular circumstances; wealth would be redistributed equally, irrespective of contribution to the social system. In this interpretation equality is a paramount value over and above all other possible values. Critics of socialist views of equality often suggest that equality of outcome is the sole objective of socialist government policy which has the consequence of destroying individual liberty (Letwin, 1983).

The notion of ontological equality does not play a significant role in contemporary social theory, because such a principle would have to be based upon a more general notion of value which would have a distinctively theological (or at least metaphysical) set of assumptions. Some Marxists would wish to assert, however, that the essence of human beings lies in their social character as 'practical, human, sensuous beings'; that is, what is common to the essence of human beings is the notion of *praxis* and it is possible to have an ontological argument about the equality of human beings (Markus, 1978). Marxists who follow the tradition of Georg Lukács tend sooner or later to consider the essence of 'Man' whereas Marx typically concerned himself with the problem of 'men' in their specific concrete and particular circumstances. It is the particularity of human beings rather than their generality which lies at the core of Marx's notion of *praxis* and social being since the social being of individuals varies according to their time and place. There is a weaker version of this argument which suggests simply that all human beings should be treated in a humane and reasonable manner as ends of activity rather than as means. Such a Kantian perspective would be entirely compatible with a strongly individualistic doctrine since the treatment of individuals as ends would be part of the essential moral outlook of an individualistic philosophy. Thus the notion that human beings are ontologically equal would have no necessary conflict with the idea that human beings are essentially individualistic and ought to be treated as separate and conscious individuals.

The paradox of the doctrine of equality of opportunity is that it leads to an inequality of consequences; it is thus often held to be philosophically incoherent as a position. Given an ideology of personal achievement, the equalization of educational opportunities would give all children a basic education but would not eradicate inequality of outcomes in a situation which emphasized competitiveness and personal aspiration. Competitive examinations in the English educational system have probably reinforced and underlined existing inequalities in society rather than contributing to their diminution (Halsey and Karabel, 1977; Halsey, Heath and Ridge, 1980). The provision of equality of opportunity in the means to achieve an education does not therefore necessarily challenge the continuity of what might be called the cultural capital of middle- and upper-class families. The continuity of inequality under circumstances of equality of opportunity would not necessarily conflict with the idea of citizenship as expressed in the work of T. H. Marshall, since this view of citizenship assumed the continuity of market economics as the main mechanism for the production of wealth in a capitalist society. In this view of citizenship what is more important is the openness of social mobility and the ability of children with talent and skill to realize their potentialities in a competitive social environment (Halsey, 1978; Heath, 1981). Furthermore, we should note that the principle of equality of opportunity is not only compatible with the traditional doctrine of individualism but actually is an essential component of such a view of human talent.

Since permissive and liberal legislation on inequality under democratic governments has not significantly changed the distribution of wealth in society or transformed the basic character of inequality, radical social theorists have sought an equality of outcome as the only genuine basis for bringing about social equality. For example, because inequality of ownership of property appears to be the root of much social disadvantage, the removal of inequality appears to require a total transformation of property rights (Becker, 1977). Thus in communist societies the attempt to realize the principle 'from each according to his abilities, to each according to his needs' has involved a massive reorganization of the total society at every level. For example, it requires a complete reorganization of property relationships so that private ownership of the effective means of production is largely obliterated (although even in communist societies in practice market forces continue to operate).

The attempt to achieve radical equality also involves a collectivization of decision-making and effort within centralized political organs in order to achieve the necessary surveillance of society as a whole. Since much human inequality is transmitted through the family system, radical social experiments under socialism have normally involved some attempt to restructure family life by, for example, separating natural from social parentage. The quest for social equality probably also involves some quite distinctive measures to break down the historic separation between the mental and manual division of labour. Socialist equality would also involve a process of re-education whereby competitive and individualistic behaviour acquired from previous social systems would be undermined through ideological reconstruction. Socialism also frequently involves an attempt to break down the rural/urban distinction and to transform the social role of the city. An equality of outcomes would also require definite attempts to prevent the emergence of bureaucratic, political and intellectual elites in the public sector; in particular, socialism would have to ensure that the offspring of any such bureaucratic leadership did not inherit the advantages of their natural parents. Finally, in order to break down the sexual division of labour it might be necessary to intervene significantly in the reproductive activities of men and women. Although the experience of socialist societies in establishing social mobility and social equality has been highly variable, the empirical evidence on existing socialist societies (at least state socialist societies) indicates the continuity of political inequality, a hierarchy of prestige, the accumulation of cultural advantages by elite groups and significant inequalities between ethnic groups and religious minorities despite attempts to achieve equality of outcome (Lane, 1971; Parkin, 1972; Giddens, 1973; Giddens and Held, 1982). The continuity of ethnic, cultural and religious minorities in Russia and China has been one illustration of the absence of civil rights. There is also the continuity of social and regional inequalities under centralized socialist conditions; the political control of minority groups such as the Kurds, Turks, Muslims and Protestant sects would be an illustration of these issues (Caroe, 1967; Bourdeaux, 1968; Chaliand, 1980; Israeli, 1980).

If we assume that the goal of equality of outcome is feasible, we might still be forced to argue that socialist governments would have to choose between this principle of equality and the principle of individual freedom. The search for radical equality appears to involve very significant interventions in the private organization of citizens' activities such that fundamental equality appears to be incompatible with fundamental freedoms. Of course, this argument presupposes a division between private and public which is historically significant in both capitalist and socialist environments. However, my conception of privacy does not necessarily involve a culturally specific or individualistic conception of privacy. The main issue is that private choices have to be constrained by social arrangements in order to bring about an aggregate equality of outcomes. One powerful illustration of this problem is to be found in the population policies of contemporary China which constrain women to bearing one offspring each; the aim of securing social wealth is incompatible with free choices about personal fertility since these fertility choices by women are incompatible with the collective goal of economic development (ironically along Malthusian lines).

THREE VERSIONS OF INDIVIDUALISM

It has been argued that the social notion of citizenship cannot be separated from some theory of equality since modern citizenship assumes an equal access to social resources and is defined by universal and equal participation in the sociopolitical community. It is difficult to separate debates about the rights of citizens from debates about equality. It has also been noted that some recent criticisms of the normative principle of equality suggest that any search for equality in modern society must be incompatible with a commitment to individualism as a value. Any social policy which seeks to bring about an equal distribution of resources will have to interfere with some aspects of individual right; the liberal defence of the individual tends to regard state intervention on behalf of social equality as anathema to the autonomy of the individual. The sociological analysis of citizenship will have to address the relationship between citizenship, equality and individualism; in particular, we must examine the alleged incompatibility between the growth of citizenship as a social movement and the autonomy of individual choice and consciousness.

Although it is often flatly asserted that equality is incompatible with individualism as moral doctrine, we have seen that the concept of equality can be broken down into at least three dimensions. Similarly, we need to recognize the complexity of the notion of individualism. In this discussion I propose to treat individualism as standing for three rather separate ideas and social developments (Turner, 1983). It is important to distinguish between individualism as a political doctrine of individual rights where this doctrine was associated in particular with writers like Hobbes and Locke. Individualism in this sense is equivalent to the notion of 'possessive individualism' as a defence of private property, unregulated markets, minimal political interference and civil rights in relationship to a bourgeoisie in opposition to traditional aristocratic powers (Macpherson, 1962). Individualism as a doctrine of property rights should be distinguished from the notion of individuality which is a cultural and elite ethic, asserting the importance of individual cultivation and moral development. Individuality is critical of unreflecting conformity to existing social standards, looking towards the educated individual to lead social taste and informed opinion. We can distinguish two forms of this ethic. There is an aristocratic and hierarchical version of this position in writers like Thomas Carlyle, Friedrich Nietzsche, and Percy Shelley. The aristocratic version of individuality asserts that a select few of enlightened individuals will perceive and understand the genious of their time to the exclusion of the mass, since genious and inspiration are necessarily restricted to an heroic minority. Thus in his defence of poetry, Shelley asserted that the poet was the window of any epoch. He gave classic expression to this exclusive norm of individual development and creativity. Aristocratic individuality asserts that no amount of training will convert the average person into a sensitive and creative individual. Individuals are born rather than made. By contrast, there is a liberal version of individuality which can be associated primarily with philosophers like J. S. Mill and to a lesser exent with J. J. Rousseau and Matthew Arnold. Liberal individuality suggests that education is essential to the development of human beings as individuals and that good taste and quality can be developed through strenuous and disciplined educational practices. The liberal version of individuality sought to maintain the highest cultural standards but thought that these were within the reach of the common man, given commitment and the right institutional means to develop taste and sympathy. Human beings in this sense are universally capable of cultural cultivation.

Both classical individualism and cultural individuality are entirely separate and different from the process of individuation. In modern societies (whether capitalist or socialist) the great majority of citizens will possess birth certificates, insurance numbers, passports, work permits, marriage certificates, car licenses, superannuation numbers and a variety of other forms of identification. These identifications are the index of modern individuation since they locate individuals uniquely and uniformly. Individuation, therefore, refers to the processes and apparatus which unify individuals while uniquely identifying them. The paradox of individuation is that it makes everybody the same while making everybody entirely different. Whereas individualism and individuality are typically oppositional beliefs and practices of privileged groups or classes, individuation makes the social control of large numbers of people bureaucratically feasible and politically effective. Individuation is thus seen to be a threat to the autonomy of the individual and the privacy of citizens because it is associated with the spread of surveillance and bureaucratic control. Individuation of populations is equivalent to M. Foucault's notion of the panoptic control of large urban populations through the creation of hierarchies, techniques of knowledge, standardization and means of measurement of large populations. It is fundamentally part of Adorno's 'administered society' and also a fundamental feature of what Weber intended by the metaphor of the iron cage.

We can now discuss the relationship between these three forms of individualism and the three types of equality. The individualism of Locke and Hobbes was an oppositional doctrine of a bourgeoisie which sought to challenge the traditionalism of the aristocracy. This form of individualism was very compatible with the notion of the civil rights of individual citizens in their quest for some political power to establish their position within a society undergoing capitalist development. The doctrine of individualism in the hands of liberal philosophers from Locke to Bentham was closely associated with the development of the power of merchants and capitalists; individualism and citizenship were important parts of a bourgeois ideology seeking a reform of parliamentary powers against land-owning aristocracies, absolutist monarchs and conservative churches. Political individualism was associated with religious and social individualism as a radical doctrine of protest against tradition. It clearly had many dimensions from free trade and free markets to individual conscience and private property. Individualism and civil citizenship were compatible with an emphasis on equality of opportunity – that is, with the freedom of the bourgeoisie to utilize its wealth and talent in the accumulation of merit and wealth. Possessive individualism is highly compatible with the notion of equality of opportunity and both are important versions of civic citizenship as a set of limited rights of speech and equality before the law. It is for this reason that Marxist theorists like Poulantzas tend to equate individualism with citizenship as identical doctrines but it is important to note that this is only one version of the notion of individualism.

Individuality can be regarded as a doctrine of a romantic elite in opposition to and reacting against industrialization and modernization. These authors tend to regard modernization (especially the rise of industrial urban society) as incompatible with a cultured existence. The aristocratic version of individuality is clearly opposed to any egalitarian development in society since aristocratic individualists regard the development of mass urban industrial society as an infringement upon an elitist world of cultivation and difference. Equality renders the world uniform in a way which is offensive to such individualists. Individuality emphasizes solitude and privacy; thus Nietzsche retired to the mountains of Sils Maria to contemplate the idea of 'eternal recurrence' while Heidegger retired to the seclusion of Todtnauberg to reflect upon the notion of Being. The egalitarian spirit of urban society is obviously culturally and spiritually remote from these forms of romantic seclusion.

There is however a more democratic version of individuality which is hostile to the notion of over-specialization and the restriction of human talent within the detail of the technical division of labour. In this perspective human beings lose their individuality as a consequence of the divisions brought about by capitalist labour practices within the factory system. In this perspective individuals lose their individuality because their talents are confined to mindless and limited activities. In this version true humanity is perceived as a total unity of mental and manual activity. When Marx envisaged a future socialist society he wrote about human beings who were multi-faceted in their interests and multi-dimensional in their activities. The removal of the social division of labour is part of the attempt to recapture and rediscover undifferentiated humanity. It would be possible therefore to conceive a *rapprochement* between a democratic version of individuality and the notion of ontological equality; furthermore, this reconciliation would be possible within a Marxist version of *praxis* which conceives of human beings as knowledgeable, practical and sensuous beings. This reconciliation might find its final location in the sensualism of Feuerbach for whom human beings could only transcend their alienation by rediscovering the completeness of their individuality.

Therefore, when social critics assert that there is a necessary incompatibility between individualism and equality, they are normally thinking about the intervention of the state in the life of the autonomous individual. It is the notion of equality of outcome which appears to be incompatible with individualism as the expression of individual autonomy. The egalitarian provision of social rights involves an individuation of the population in order to achieve adequate administrative and bureaucratic conditions for social justice. The spread of bureaucracy is associated with the growth of individuation as the state attempts to provide some supervision of the distribution of welfare. The development of universal franchise, the modern health system, equal provision of education and a social infrastructure for urban society required both a stable bureaucracy and a detailed form of individuation. Thus Marshall's notion of social citizenship in the twentieth century is necessarily linked with the development of an interventionist social policy which for its success requires bureaucracy and surveillance. The equality of outcome is therefore not only compatible with individuation but actually requires it in order to be successful in terms of some norm of social justice and egalitarianism. Individuation in this sense has been the object of criticism by Weber in his view of rationalization, by critical theorists in the notion of the administered society and by Foucault in his view of panoptic social systems. These criticisms are in many respects romantic and nostalgic, since they largely neglect the positive benefits of stable administration and social surveillance. These perspectives on administration may be characterized as forms of metaphysical pathos (Gouldner, 1955). Although bureaucracy has been subject to lengthy and detailed criticism in sociology and political science, bureaucracy is necessary for the successful operation of any democracy where there is a commitment to the equal, stable and reliable delivery of a uniform service (Albrow, 1970).

It is difficult to see how members of the working classes could develop their individuality, skill and talents without the public provision of education, health and security. Since they are denied the material means to seek these benefits privately through the free market, they are forced to depend upon the bureaucratic and public provision of such services. Individuation in this sense is thus necessary for the development of individuality within the democratic tradition. Individuation does not then represent so much an invasion of the state but the enablement of individuals to achieve and satisfy their individual aims. Individuation provides the baseline from which individuals could launch into individuality. While the public sector is criticized for its inefficiency, its bureaucracy and its intrusion in individual life, the substantial improvements in general health and education in postwar Britain would have been impossible without state intervention and without individuation. At least we should recognize the paradox of individuation. First, it makes the social and political surveillance of large numbers of people possible; it is thus obviously a threat to individual autonomy. This is the Orwellian version of individuation as the obliteration of personal difference. Secondly, individuation provides a uniform basis for individual development and contributes to the creativity and individuality of the person. It provides the basis for the cultivation of the individual in a context of inequality via the market place. The expansion of social rights in the twentieth century would have been impossible without state intervention through the mechanism of bureaucratic individuation.

RATIONALIZATION AND PERSONALITY

In one respect to be a citizen is to have personality, since citizenship involves rights and responsibilities; only an individual with personality is capable of responsibility, because one traditional dividing line between humanity and animality is the question of rational responsibility. To be a full citizen is to be an individual equipped with personality and thus a capacity for rational choice and obligation. One feature of the pessimistic view of bureaucracy, mass democracy and rational administration is that modern society is impersonal and depersonalizes human existence. Thus the spread of the iron cage reduces the capacity for personality and undermines the responsible dimension of citizenship as the status of a rational being. Max Weber's pessimistic view of history would carry with it the implication of diminishing citizenship with increasing bureaucracy, rational society and the secularization of values.

This perspective on the fatalistic consequences of history has an important consequence for Weber's theoretical analysis of the character of action and social action with respect to personality. Weber distinguished four types of social action: namely, instrumentally rational action, value rational action, affectual action and traditional action. Affectual and traditional actions are on the borderline between what is meaningful action and what is mere behaviour. Weber wanted to reserve the idea of action for activities which are aimed at well-formulated goals, involving human subjectivity and the ascription of meaning. Traditional action by contrast is characterized by what Weber regarded as mere habituation, and affectual behaviour involved emotionally charged activity and was on the borderline between behaviour and action. The peculiarity of this theoretical stance is that, as Weber himself was aware, everyday activity is activity which is essentially habitual, routine and unreflecting. Therefore, the everyday world lies to some extent outside the interests of a sociology of action and ordinary life is an arena where interpretive sociology has little purchase. Everyday life is a phenomenon suitable to the approach of behaviourism. The mundane world of ordinary people is a space dominated by habit, tradition and emotion whereas the notion of action applies to moral activity and interpretive sociology applies to a reality characterized by intention and reflexivity. It is in this area that we can fully grasp the Kantian legacy of Weber's sociological perspective since the idea of action would only apply to human beings equipped with personality, that is with intention, consciousness and moral insight. This routine and mundane world is in Weber's historical sociology periodically disrupted by major religious movements, by charismatic leaders and by social movements under the stimulus of ideas relating to salvation. In these historical terms it was the ascetic Protestant and the Jewish prophet who transformed themselves in the process of challenging the world.

To have personality in these terms is to act rationally – that is, in terms of ends which are ethical and self-consciously formulated. To have personality is to have a project in life rather than being merely determined by the chance circumstances of nature and society. Personality lies at the social end of the continuum between reason and nature, since personality involves the denial or control over emotion, habit and feeling. Personality involves moral choice and the rejection of the natural world. For Weber, human existence was degraded by what he regarded as an average ethic and it was the duty of the morally committed individual to seek heroic rejection of nature and society. In this sense an individual was a person with a vocation or calling in life and a personality is an agent with a vocation to change the habituation of ordinary life and to defy the psychological laws of nature (Brubaker, 1984).

Because Weber's sociology is based upon historical and comparative assumptions, it is important to ask under what historical circumstances personality is most likely to develop and further to enquire what set of circumstances has the effect of diminishing personality. In Weber's viewpoint one would want to suggest that personality develops as a consequence of Protestant Christianity and industrial capitalism, since these two historical changes liberated the human agent from the control of emotion and tradition. It was western capitalism which destroyed magic, the stability of the rural community, the dominance of church practices and the control of social life by habit and custom. Capitalism tore up the tranquillity of rural existence and pushed the individual into history. If capitalism creates the moral individual, it also undermines personality by subordinating the human agent to the regimentation of the factory, the rationalization by science, the routines of capitalist production and the mundane reality of the division of labour. Since we inhabit a world without clear and absolute moral guidelines, it is difficult to see how anybody could raise themselves to the level of personality. Max Weber's notion of the ethic of responsibility seems unable to provide a realistic solution to value relativity in the modern world and, regardless of arguments to the contrary, this ethic appears to suggest merely that we should approach the world realistically, facing adversity with calmness. This seriousness of moral purpose is however hardly a calling to a life grounded in deliberation, rational organization and planning as an effort to overcome the traditional character of the mundane world.

From Weber's view of the history of rationalization it would appear that personality had a relatively limited existence; personality emerged as a consequence of social changes in the seventeenth century but, with the development of bureaucratic rational society, personality became increasingly subordinated by the state, by science and by bureaucratic surveillance. Personality has a tragic history, being obliterated by the very circumstances that created it in the first instance. This theme of the vanishing personality follows directly from Weber's pessimistic view of history and his nostalgic concern for early capitalism as an age of heroism. It is also an effect of his elitist morality with its emphasis on aristocratic individuality; it is the ethical virtuosi who pull themselves to the stature of moral agents by transforming their own lives by moral purpose. However, Weber's position creates a logical puzzle since sociology becomes increasingly irrelevant in a world dominated by habit, if we define sociology as the science of action. However, there is no reason for adopting Weber's pessimistic view of the world and we are not compelled to accept the idea that somehow the life of habit and sentiment is blind or that personality resides exclusively in reason which challenges and controls the life of feeling and emotion. At a more technical level we could challenge the idea that habit and tradition involved little or no element of choice or interpretation. What counts as habit is not a fact of nature but itself the outcome of interpretation and purpose. All actions are deeply contextual and what counts as habit in one social setting may not count as habit in another; habit involves judgement in the sense of interpretation. A similar position might be mounted against the notion of personality since in everyday conversation to say that someone has 'personality' is to imply that they are somewhat unusual or peculiar, being not regulated by habit. The concept of personality in psychology, by contrast, is employed more in terms of specifying regular occurrences of behaviour. Thus the idea of personality may refer to entirely different areas of human activity and the coherence of concept itself is historically produced. The very notion of personality is an outcome of the historical transformation of the notion of *persona* as a collective mask in classical society (Mauss, 1979).

The issue of personality in classical sociology was ultimately grounded in a view of reality which has strong romantic and pessimistic elements. Regardless of Weber's own hostility to romanticism, there is in his sociology a romantic attachment to rationality, since for Weber rationality involved an heroic act worked out against the mundane world. This view of rational action is associated with a virtuoso ethic where only heroes have real personalities. Weber, like Nietzsche, was attached to an aristocratic individuality in which great personalities struggle in history against meaninglessness. Weber could not adequately appreciate the rationality of habit which for ordinary people typically involves their heroic struggle against deprivation, ill health, uncertainty and political suppression. Habit can in this sense be regarded as the accumulated wisdom of ordinary people struggling for a place in history and society. It is thus perfectly rational for the common man to adhere to habit as a defensive structure. In the anthropological sense, human culture is the accumulated residue of such rational adaptation to the contingency of ordinary life. Our existence in the world is made possible by this accumulated and habitual reason. It is interesting in this respect to reflect on Kant's own life which was totally regulated and habitual. It was said that the housewives of Königsberg would set their clocks by Kant's private walk and routine. This entirely habitual reality was the necessary context for the heroic struggle of Kant's mind to grapple with the problem of nature and reason. Thus habit and a principled moral life are not mutually incompatible.

WHAT IS A PERSON?

This critique of Weber's notion of personality in fact drives us to a more complex and difficult set of issues concerning the nature of the person. In this study of citizenship we have seen that a number of contemporary social movements which exhibit a concern for nature have pushed the problem of citizenship into the realm of inanimate phenomena. These social movements have raised questions about whether animals have a legal status as personalities and similar movements related to feminist issues have raised questions about the status of embryos as persons. The problem of the emergence of personality in history as a consequence of religious and economic changes is thus closely bound up with a traditional philosophical issue – namely, what is to count as a person. Although there is much disagreement in contemporary philosophy about the definition of such concepts as the self, the individual and the person, any comprehensive definition of person would have to take into account the following: the body; the consciousness; continuity and commitment; and rationality, choice and responsibility.

In discussing the importance of the body for the definition of persons, philosophers typically point out that in a person's lifetime their body changes almost totally and therefore it is difficult to see how the body as flux could define or be relevant to something relatively stable such as the person. Conventional philosophy also notes that parts of the body can be cut off without there being any question as to the identity of the person whose body is being gradually amputated. While these are perfectly valid philosophical objections, the body appears to be quite crucial to the definition of the person in sociology since in routine situations we identify persons with respect to their physical presentation of themselves, that is through their bodies. Although these physical characteristics of the body are never an absolutely certain guide to identity, because there are mistaken identities, false identities and assumed identities, the body is nevertheless crucial to the social and political location of persons. Moreover, the body is never simply a physical entity but a system of symbols involving characteristics, postures, manifestations and locations. In the words of Goffman, we are always presenting ourselves through our bodies. Having a body as a unique location and characterization of ourselves is important in the debate about citizenship, since, for example, our fingerprints may be quite crucial to our social and political status and identity.

Therefore, the body is quite paradoxical in many respects (Turner, 1984b). The body can also have a fictive identity as in the case of mediaeval theory that kings had two bodies (Foucault, 1977). The king's sacred body was the symbol of the unity of the body politic while his earthly body was simply a manifestation of his mundane existence. The notion of the continuity of the political system was often embodied by the burial effigy of the king after death. Furthermore, the notion of the body of Christ provided one of the early metaphors for the development of the notion of legal corporation where trading companies in mediaeval times were assumed to have fictive bodies which were greater than the sum of their parts. In a modern company the shareholders constitute a legal body and under laws of limited liability it is the corporation, and not the individual members, which is held legally responsible for its actions. The growth of multinational corporations has raised rather complex and vexed legal questions relating to the notion of an international body which transcends the legislative authority of any given nation-state. Thus in contemporary society there are a variety of collective subjects such as public bodies, trusts and insurance companies which are legal subjects but not necessarily human persons despite their legal personality. As we have already noted, one consequence of modern movements such as feminism and environmentalism is that the corporal status of citizens has become incredibly complex. It is no longer clear in what sense natural parents own their own plasma and genetic inheritance. Many of the crucial debates about citizenship which will occupy modern societies undoubtedly focus on the status of fertilized embryos as quasi-persons and thus quasi-citizens.

Although embodiment is crucial to identity and to social membership, philosophers and sociologists have normally turned to forms of subjectivity to define what constitutes a person especially as a social actor. Thus questions of memory, consciousness, knowledge and personal definition are prominent in the notion of what it is to be a person and a responsible citizen. Since citizens are held to be responsible for their actions, they must be knowledgeable and conscious. Traditionally, it was this moral consciousness as incorporated in language and symbol which was held to distinguish human beings from animals. Thus loss of memory may be highly damaging for anyone wishing to claim the rights and privileges of a citizen.

One useful definition of personal identity in sociology runs as follows (Kavolis, 1980, p. 41):

(1) the perception of an overal coherence – either 'substantive' or 'methodological' – within the experiences and expressions of an individual;
(2) the memory of this individual and, normally, in at least some others of the *continuity* of the 'story' – or 'tale' – of his life; and
(3) a conscious, but not wholly conscious, *commitment* to a particular manner of both comprehending and managing one's own self.

The coherence and stability of a person's social identity are bound up with the coherence of their beliefs, actions and experiences but this coherence is both intrapsychic and intersocial. We recognize the coherence of our own personalities with respect to the appraisal of other social actors. In practice, being the same person is measured by the fact that we behave in the same way over time and this sameness is routinely confirmed by our contemporaries. In short, being the same person is being defined as the same person by our consociates. The continuity of the person is, at least in part, guaranteed by the state as a legal consociate which guarantees and confirms our identity via such documentary evidence as the passport.

Human beings are above all defined as agents who are responsible for their actions and are therefore capable of obligation and trust. The state operates as the provider of protection and security in exchange for the loyalty and obligation of the subjects who are capable of rational choice and decision-making. Citizens are agents capable of contracts. There are of course interesting sociological paradoxes in the argument that rationality and responsibility are defining characteristics of human persons. At various times women, children and lunatics have been excluded from citizenship on the grounds that they are incapable of rational choice and responsibility. This was particularly important in the case of women who on marriage lost their legal status. Under the legal system of *coverture* which evolved in European feudalism and was fully organized by the time of the sixteenth century, a woman ceased to be a legal person on marriage because her identity was submerged in that of her husband. This erosion and erasure were fully operative in Britain until the passing of various matrimonial causes Acts, starting in 1857. These legal changes in the status of women came about because the family was no longer central to the conservation of property, because with the growth of political individualism it was difficult to exclude women on the particular grounds of their gender and because the new family laws made the legal involvement of women in the courts financially and legally possible. Above all the transformation of the status of women was brought about by the feminist movement at both a political and social level. Historically, however, women were a category of persons who were strictly speaking not persons and were thus excluded from the public domain of rational action.

The expansion of social citizenship in the nineteenth and twentieth centuries thus involves an expansion of the category of what is to count as a person. The emancipation of women and children involves attributing legal personality to them; any expansion of animal rights in a sense attributes personality to animals. The state clearly plays a major part in identifying and stabilizing such legal subjects. This has led some Marxists to draw a parallel between the Christian God and the modern state since God as the Subject creates his earthly and individual subjects; so the modern state through an act of legal will creates the citizen as a social subject. Thus legal ideology interpellates the individual as a subject and conditions and subordinates the subject to the

Subject (the state) (Althusser, 1971). Having constituted subjects, official ideology then inserts them within the positions and practices of a society where they accept their obligations voluntarily and contentedly. This particular version of interpellation in the writing of Poulantzas (1978) reduces individuals to merely political parrots. These structuralist interpretations of the person deny consciousness and subjectivity which are necessary conditions for an individual to identify a message sent by the Subject. To be interpellated a person must possess consciousness in order to identify messages from the state correctly. Furthermore, writers like Althusser do not recognize different interpellations (of gender, ethnicity, nationality or occupational status) or how these might be related. There could be, and there are, contradictory locations and identifications for subjects. Of course, subjects do not always (and not unequivocally) respond to hailing (Urry, 1981). Furthermore, dominant forms of interpellation will always generate an anti-ideology of resistance and opposition (Therborn, 1980). It is precisely because citizens as persons possess self-reflexive consciousness that they are capable of resistance as well as capable of obligation and responsibility. Citizens who possess literacy are capable of reading and following government instructions but by the same token they are capable of reading subversive and revolutionary literature. This was the classic problem faced by the Sunday School movement in the nineteenth century that teaching its subjects to read the Bible also equipped them to read revolutionary tracts.

INDIVIDUAL VERSES CITIZEN: THE FINAL PARADOX

The evolution of the subjective person is to some extent also the history of western rational society. The gradual decline of feudal society brought the self out of the social role and cultivated the personality on the basis of education and skill rather than blood and ascriptive criteria. The *persona* became increasingly subjective and expressive with the gradual disappearance of the mask, the shield and external symbols as physical carriers of the social self. With the emergence of the modern period, the social self was now equipped with knowledge, consciousness, a soul and individuality but not all subjective persons were social and political citizens. This development of the subjective self was intimately bound up with the development of etiquette at the court, new manners of sociality and patterns of intimacy; the court provided the opening for the development ultimately of the intimate space of the new bourgeoisie (Elias, 1983). In the seventeenth century, capitalism combined itself with individualism as the ideological legitimation of property but capitalism also produced (via new exchange relationships and markets) a series of universalistic norms of social worth and entitlement; it was to these social rights that radical movements appealed in their critique and opposition to social inequalities based upon inheritance and ascription. There is obviously an agreement in political theory that civil rights may be politically conservative as a mere abatement of class conflict but once these civil rights have been successfully combined with political and social rights it becomes increasingly plausible to suggest that there is an incompatibility between the market interest of competitive capitalism and the inroads of social citizenship into private profit.

One consequence of the development of universalistic forms of citizenship has been the gradual liquidation of ascriptive definitions of the person since gender, age and ethnicity become progressively irrelevant for the continuity of capitalist production. Gender is not a requirement for the continuity of capitalism in the workplace and in the household, since capitalism operates successfully with or without such specifications. Indeed modern capitalism tends to undermine patriarchy and other forms of hierarchy both within the family and in the workplace. It is clear that industrial societies, as a matter of fact, do have massive income inequality with respect to gender; however, the main reason we can say that income levels are unequal is precisely because we have such universalistic standards to which we can appeal in order to make the critique. In the language of Marxism, capitalist society produces individualism as a doctrine which hails the legal person on a universalistic basis. Such persons become increasingly abstract, general and cosmopolitan. At the same time in order to provide services on a universalistic basis, the state intervenes in society and the result is a bureaucratic individuation of the individual. The paradox is that capitalism develops individualism while also requiring individuation; individualism is an oppositional critique of public surveillance, while individuation is the necessary basis for the surveillance of subjects as citizens.

As the waves of citizenship move outwards as a consequence of social movement to achieve real rights, the particularistic criteria which define the person become increasingly irrelevant in the public sphere. The ontological puzzle is whether there will prove to be real persons lying behind the multiple layers of particularity – that is, to be a person is always to be a particular person; one is defined by unique ascriptive, local, accidental and personal features. To be a citizen is to be defined by general, abstract, bureaucratic and public criteria relevant to such issues as taxation, political control and education. There appears to be a paradox that individuals require particularity, while citizens require generality. Yet it is the growth of individualism which is closely associated with the development of modern citizenship. Equally it is the development of citizenship which has created the basis for the development of individuality on the part of educated, self-conscious, reflective agents.

6
Conclusion

THEORETICAL SUMMARY

Citizenship may be defined in a variety of ways (by reference to civil, legal and social features) but citizenship rights are essentially concerned with the nature of social participation of persons within the community as fully recognized legal members. Citizenship expands with the boundaries which contain society so that the more limited the nature of society the more limited the nature of citizenship rights. In premodern societies citizenship was restricted to a small group of men who were typically property owners and who controlled the political process by virtue of their wealth. Slaves, women and children were excluded by virtue of their dependent status on property owners as bearers of political rights. Political rights were exclusionary and controlled access to resources. By contrast, obligations were restricted to those who performed duties on behalf of the citizenry within a city-state. While these political systems often had a democratic element at least in terms of procedures, democracy was circumscribed by the narrow conception of citizenship. The terrain which lay outside this circumscribed political entity may be defined as 'nature', as that phenomenon which stands against the social arena. The implication is that the expansion of society brings about a contraction and blurring of the distinction between society/nature. Women were outside society and citizenship because they were natural agents concerned with the reproduction of men rather than with the reproduction of culture.

Bourgeois revolutions against conservative feudal powers from the seventeenth century onwards involved an attack on the exclusionary privileges of the aristocracy in the name of individual rights especially individual rights of property, freedom of association, and parliamentary rights. In the early definition of liberal politics access to parliament was founded upon an individual view of property and the bourgeois definition of social membership contained an attack upon the ascriptive privileges of blood in the name of cultivation of personality. Writers like Hobbes, Locke and Halifax gave expression to this new political code in terms of a theory of social contract by which the rational individual was bound to the community as a consequence of consent. These theories were largely individualistic, secular and expedient; state-craft was about reconciling conflicting interests within the political market-place, just as market society was dominated by the exchange of commodities by rational producers and consumers of goods.

The French Revolution gave rise to a new inquiry into the relationship between equality and liberty within a republican political framework. The consequences of this political revolution involved a new conceptualization of women in relationship to citizenship, a new concern for the character of Jewish liberation and an appreciation of the social dimension of equality rather than the natural dimensions of inequality. The growth of citizenship is strongly connected with the emergence of capitalism, the French Revolution and the development of nationalism as a dominant ideological system. Citizenship gave expression to the new forces of bourgeois individualism, political administration via bureaucracy and the emergence of nationalism as the key to political identity. Citizenship at this stage was primarily about civil and political rights for an urban bourgeoisie in the context of the developing secular states of Europe and North America. Citizenship is a radical and socially disruptive process whereby, through a series of expanding processes, social membership becomes increasingly universalistic and open-ended.

The movement of citizenship is from the particular to the universal, since particular definitions of persons for the purpose of exclusion appear increasingly irrational and incongruent with the basis of the modern polity. The expansion of citizenship is from ascription to achievement. The development of citizenship is also from the hierarchical to the horizontal, so that fixed positions of a formal status system begin to dissolve under the impact of universalistic democratic rights of citizenship. It is for this reason that citizenship provides us with a measure of modernization, where modernization involves the collapse of legitimate systems of patriarchy, gerontocracy and patrimonialism. These hierarchical structures are replaced by naked competition in the market place where classes and other occupational groups seek through exclusionary practices to preserve their privileged access to resources. These market practices are also subject to criticism from democratic citizenship where forms of positive discrimination are mobilized to seek a redress between advantaged and disadvantaged groups. The growth of modernity is a movement from de-jure inequalities in terms of legitimate status hierarchies to de-facto inequalities as a consequence of naked market forces where the labourer is defined as a 'free' person.

The claims to individual rights which were first used by the bourgeoisie against the aristocracy are now used by workers against employers, by women against men, by children's advocates against parents and by migrant workers against their host communities. Citizenship rights are not simply empty civil rights which are utilized to reinforce existing inequalities. Although bourgeois freedoms did not address the underlying inequality of the market place, in contemporary society the notion of social citizenship is frequently and typically employed as a critique of capitalism via the welfare state. The expansion of citizenship is at the cost of profitability and hierarchical authoritarian control in the polity, the enterprise and the home.

There are various processes within modern society which tend to bring about citizenship through establishing forms of egalitarian social relationships. These include social and geographical mobility, an achievement-oriented education system, a public means of mass communication and a consumer economy. The general conditions of social egalitarianism foster political and social citizenship as the predominant framework of political action. The struggle for citizenship by social movements and subordinate groups, however, is contingent and reversible, since the erosion of profitability will always lead to a strong response from the owners of capital.

Capitalist society like all other forms of human social organization is inherently contradictory as a social system. The conflict between equality as an aspect of citizenship and market forces in the form of class relationships is one such contradiction which may be expressed more elegantly by saying that in capitalist systems the political process is disjoined from the economic base of society with the result that the politics of equality conflicts with the economics of inequality.

Whether or not citizenship provides the ultimate institutional support for the continuity of capitalism is primarily an empirical question which should be addressed by sociological research rather than being specified in advance. However, it seems perfectly plausible to believe that citizenship (especially in terms of civil and legal rights) supports the continuity of the capitalist mode of production by giving expression to bourgeois requirements in the market place and also that citizenship supports capitalism in the sense of providing some form of abatement of direct conflict between groups. This position is perfectly in line with Marshall's view of the role of such bourgeois freedoms as the right to own property. However, we can also argue that citizenship undermines the capacity of private capitalist enterprises to realize their investment through profits since the expansion of social rights is translated into increased taxation, state regulation of the market and legislation to control the inheritance of property.

THE COSTS OF CITIZENSHIP

The purpose of this contribution to the controversy surrounding working-class action inside capitalist society is to lend support to a view cogently presented by John Rex that the study of social conflict should be central to sociology as such (Rex, 1981). Capitalist society has been analysed in terms of the endless conflict not only of classes but of social groups, social strata and social movements where these conflicts hinge on the distribution of resources in the name of social rights. The consequences of the conflict are contingent and contradictory.

All social institutions have contradictory consequences. It is neither the case that citizenship always supports the stability of capitalism, nor that it inevitably undermines it. In most situations a variety of consequences of social institutions is to be expected. One typical illustration (albeit an inherently tragic one) would be the role of the gun laws in the USA. The constitutional right of the citizen to bear arms had a strong egalitarian and democratic element while also reinforcing the importance of local autonomy and local government. However, in the contemporary context the easy availability of arms fosters a culture of violence which undermines the freedom of individuals to associate in public without fear and intimidation. A variety of interest groups manipulate these regulations relating to arms in a way which is utterly cynical as a defence of their own profit.

The development of citizenship has been bought at a certain social cost. One such cost is the expansion of bureaucracy, surveillance and public regulation over the citizen. The attempt to deliver a uniform service through welfare institutions inevitably leads to an increase in bureaucracy and control through the individuation of legal personalities. While this obviously promotes an 'administered society', this study has not accepted the pessimistic critique of bureaucracy which is implicit in the sociology of Weber, Adorno and Foucault. Where there is a political commitment to providing a service on an egalitarian basis to a mass of the population there will be inevitably an increase in officialdom, bureaucracy and public control, but the resulting improvement in the general standards of living for this population is an acceptable price of bureaucracy given a moral commitment to some form of substantive justice. Furthermore, we do not have to accept the implicit resignation in Weber's notion of the iron cage, since the appropriate response would be to seek ways of making bureaucracy more responsive to individual, local or group requirements. If the alternative to rational bureaucracy is ad-hoc administration, it appears reasonable to accept a high degree of bureaucracy in the interests of stability of service. Equality demands standards, standards require regulation and regulation can be most effectively achieved by bureaucracy. The social world of both late capitalism and state socialism depends upon an intensive regulation of persons by the process of individuation which separates out individuals in order to achieve more detailed and more stable administration.

Although citizenship developed before capitalism, the expansion of capitalism gave rise to an expansion of citizenship through an extension of exchange relationships within the market place. The growth of citizenship at the capitalist core was associated with a reduction of rights at the periphery as a consequence of the explosion of capitalist commodities within traditional markets under exploitative, concessionary arrangements (Turner, 1984a). The consequence of capitalist expansion was to impose white-settler colonialism on peripheral and subordinate social systems with the consequent displacement of aboriginal populations to regions of little or no agricultural value. Capitalism led to an erosion of these aboriginal rights in a period when working-class social movements were securing greater social welfare. There was also a development of internal colonialism whereby marginal social groups in peripheral regions within the capitalist societies were being subordinated. Capitalism is inherently uneven in its development and brings about advances in certain social sectors while requiring exploitation, domination and displacement in others. However, as Marx and Engels noted, colonialism had contradictory consequences in liquidating hierarchy, tradition, religious culture and premodern institutions through the impact of private property and market relationships (Avineri, 1970; Turner, 1974b, 1977). Colonial institutions, like all other social institutions, had highly uneven and contradictory consequences with respect to the expansion and contraction of social rights. However, the struggle against white colonialism has often been equipped with the ideological armament of citizenship as an ideology – that is, opponents of racism typically appeal to notions of universalism and egalitarianism which are essential to citizenship.

One crucial problem for citizenship rights is the relationship between citizenship and the nation-state. The development of modern citizenship has corresponded to the development of a system of nation-states within a capitalist economic system. Within this nation-state context it is typically the case that people without a country fall between a number of political systems with the consequence that they have no rights for political membership. Citizenship is often exclusionary as a system of protective rights against aliens but alien status is itself the outcome of unresolved conflict and struggle. The Kurds would be a primary illustration of this conflict between citizenship and national identity, where Kurds as a group live under a variety of regimes in Syria, Iraq, Iran and Turkey. In general, pastoral nomads have fared badly under modern political and economic conditions where state security is often seen to be threatened by their mobility. Although the modern economy is global, the political systems of the world are national and thus we have a system of national citizenship in a social context which requires a new theory of internationalism and universalistic citizenship. Political attempts to create a more universalistic notion of citizenship – whether through the League of Nations, the European Economic Community, the Helsinki Accord or the United Nations – have been generally unsuccessful. Indeed there are strong pressures towards subregional and local political identities which often rule out a larger political commitment to supranationalist entities. This problem is an ancient issue and was the core problem in Marx's treatment of the Jewish Question. Since racism is ubiquitous, suppressed and exploited groups may well find a nationalist/territorial solution their only realistic hope for survival and nationalist struggles for rights are by definition exclusionary. The conflict between Zionist and Palestinian nationalism is characteristic of this crisis of national citizenship as an exclusionary struggle for access to limited resources. The growth of abstract social rights within a nation-state context may well lead to a diminution or abolition of rights for minority groups where these groups fall outside an exclusionary political definition of membership.

AGAINST NOSTALGIA

The critique of capitalism often implies either implicitly or covertly a nostalgic view of precapitalist systems in which there was a relatively low division of labour, a sense of community and a more open expression of emotion and feeling. Premodern societies are often seen to be morally coherent because they are based on a set of shared values prior to the emergence of class relationships (MacIntyre, 1967a and b). There was also an implicit nostalgia in Weber's dominant metaphors of rationalization, where he often depicted capitalism in terms of a loss of grace.

Rational capitalism lacks meaning because we have eaten from the Tree of Knowledge and we have discovered that we are *sans* figs. By contrast, Marx recognized the paradoxically progressive element of capitalism in destroying the vegetative nature of village life, undermining the humbug of feudal belief systems, destroying the hierarchical relationships of privilege and status, freeing the peasant from the local constraints of custom and exchange, and finally creating a cosmopolitan environment through the exchange of commodities on a world market. Although Marx also recognized the inherently exploitative and bloody nature of this capitalist history, he nevertheless regarded capitalism as progressive. Capitalism brings people into history and creates the conditions for a radical transformation of consciousness and practice, but at a massive social and personal cost.

In addition to its nostalgia, sociology is – at least classically – fatalistic. Sociology like traditional economics is a dismal science and this pessimistic mood is essential to much of the sociology of bureaucracy, anomie, alienation, industrialization and secularization. Weber's sociology as a whole was an expression of fate where fatalism was basic to his analysis of the unintended consequences of action. In Weber's sociology we have a narrative structure in which good intentions inevitably have bad consequences. The Weberian analysis of Protestantism is the central episode in this historic fatalism, since the good intentions of salvation have the bad consequences of capitalism. Although that is an over-simplified account, it does capture the pessimistic mood of Weber's sociology in which rationality collapses into meaninglessness and individualism descends into bureaucracy. Our mastery of the world leads to our enslavement in the cage of reason. In Marx we might discover the opposite of Weber in the sense that bad intentions have unintended beneficial consequences. Although capitalism is inherently violent and exploitative, it creates a context in which progressive forces may develop and where an enhancement of human reason and experience becomes possible. Citizenship exists despite rather than because of capitalist growth. The autonomy of the market (despite the relative nature of that autonomy) from culture, social structure and politics creates a space where individualism, universalism, contractual relationships and secularity can develop. The ideological defence of this market by the bourgeoisie against feudal powers in terms of an ideology of property rights was ultimately turned against the bourgeoisie by working classes which mobilized bourgeois culture in defence of equal social rights and the benefits of welfare. Capitalism creates the condition for its own demise and transcendence in that the conditions for socialism grow out of the struggle for genuine rights in capitalism. The anarchy of the market place creates the conditions for the development of the state as that institution which guarantees social contracts and provides an administration within which profits can be realized but the state also becomes an institution necessary for the protection and development of social rights. Capitalism is transformed by a set of institutions which were designed to maintain and protect its continuity. The state in capitalist society is popular rather than bourgeois in the sense that the state arises from popular conflict and struggle to enlarge and democratize state institutions against the interests of capital. The classical Marxist question (namely, why the working classes are not revolutionary) is inadequately posed (Urry, 1981). The Marxist commentary on reformism assumes that capitalist societies have remained largely unchanged and that, since these societies are still capitalist, the proletariat should be revolutionary. However, capitalism has changed at least partly as a result of popular working-class conflict and continues to change as a result of the social struggles of a variety of social movements which are not class-based.

References

Abercrombie, N., Hill, S., and Turner, B. S. (1980), *The Dominant Ideology Thesis* (London: Allen & Unwin).
Abercrombie, N., and Urry, J. (1983), *Capital, Labour and the Middle Classes* (London: Allen & Unwin).
Alavi, H., and Shanin, T. (eds) (1982), *Introduction to the Sociology of 'Developing Societies'* (London: Macmillan).
Albrow, M. (1970), *Bureaucracy* (London: Pall Mall Press).
Alexander, J. C. (1982), *Theoretical Logic in Sociology, Positivism, Presuppositions and Controversies*, Vol. 1 (London: Routledge & Kegan Paul).
Althusser, L. (1971), *Lenin, Philosophy and Other Essays* (London: New Left Books).
Althusser, L., and Balibar, E. (1970), *Reading Capital* (London: New Left Books).
Amin, S. (1974), *Accumulation on a World Scale: A Critique of the Theory of Underdevelopment* (London: Harvester Press).
Amin, S. (1976), *Unequal Development: An Essay on the Social Formations of Peripheral Capitalism* (London: Harvester Press).
Anderson, P. (1964), 'Origins of the present crisis', *New Left Review*, no. 23, pp. 26–53.
Anderson, P. (1974), *Lineages of the Absolutist State* (London: New Left Books).
Apter, D. E. (1965), *The Politics of Modernization* (Chicago: Chicago University Press).
Ariés, P. (1973), *Centuries of Childhood* (Harmondsworth: Penguin).
Aristotle (1962), *The Politics* (with an introduction by T. A. Sinclair) (Harmondsworth: Penguin).
Avineri, S. (1970), *The Social and Political Thought of Karl Marx* (London: Cambridge University Press).
Ball, R. J., and Doyle, P. (1969), *Inflation* (Harmondsworth: Penguin).
Banks, J. A. (1972), *The Sociology of Social Movements* (London: Macmillan).
Barrett, M., and McIntosh, M. (1982), *The Anti-Social Family* (London: Verso).
Becker, L. C. (1977), *Property Rights* (London: Routledge & Kegan Paul).
Bell, D. (1976), *The Cultural Contradictions of Capitalism* (London: Heinemann).
Berger, M. (1967), *Equality by Statute: The Revolution in Civic Rights* (New York: Doubleday).
Berghe, P. L. van der (1983), 'Ethnic melting pots or plural societies',

Australian and New Zealand Journal of Sociology, vol. 19, no. 2, pp. 238–52.
Berlin, I. (1978), *Karl Marx, His Life and Environment* (Oxford: Oxford University Press).
Béteille, A. (1983), *The Idea of Natural Inequality and Other Essays* (Delhi: Oxford University Press).
Blackwell, E. (1977), *Opening the Medical Profession to Women* (New York: Schocken).
Bottomore, T. B. (1971), 'Class structure and social consciousness' in Istvan Mészáros (ed.), *Aspects of History and Consciousness* (London: Merlin Press), pp. 49–64.
Bottomore, T. B. (1975), *Sociology as Social Criticism* (London: Allen & Unwin).
Bottomore, T. B. (1979), *Political Sociology* (London: Hutchinson).
Bottomore, T. B. (1984a), *The Frankfurt School* (Chichester: Ellis Horwood; London: Tavistock).
Bourdeaux, M. (1968), *Religious Ferment in Russia* (London: Macmillan).
Brotz, H. M. (1964), *The Black Jews of Harlem: Negro Nationalism and the Dilemma of Negro Leadership* (New York: Schocken).
Brown, M. B. (1972), *From Labourism to Socialism* (London: Spokesman).
Brubaker, R. (1984), *The Limits of Rationality: An Essay on the Social and Moral Thought of Max Weber* (London: Allen & Unwin).
Brym, R. J. (1980), *Intellectuals and Politics* (London: Allen & Unwin).
Burke, P. (1980), *Sociology and History* (London: Allen & Unwin).
Burrage, M. (1969), 'Culture and British economic growth', *British Journal of Sociology*, vol. 20, pp. 117–33.
Burrow, J. W. (1970), *Evolution and Society: A Study in Victorian Social Theory* (London: Cambridge University Press).
Carlebach, J. (1978), *Karl Marx and the Radical Critique of Judaism* (London: Routledge & Kegan Paul).
Carnoy, M. (1984), *The State and Political Theory* (Princeton, NJ: Princeton University Press).
Caroe, D. (1967), *Soviet Empire, the Turks of Central Asia and Stalinism* (New York: St Martin's Press).
Castells, M. (1977), *The Urban Question* (London: Edward Arnold).
Castells, M. (1978), *City, Class and Power* (London: Macmillan).
Castles, S., and Kosack, G. (1973), *Immigrant Workers and Class Structure in Western Europe* (London: Oxford University Press).
Chaliand, G. (1980), *People Without a Country, the Kurds and Kurdistan* (London: Zed Press).
Charvet, J. (1974), *The Social Problem in the Philosophy of Rousseau* (Cambridge: Cambridge University Press).
Cobban, A. (1961), *A History of Modern France*, 2 vols. (Harmondsworth: Penguin).
Cohen, P. S. (1968), *Modern Social Theory* (London: Heinemann).

References

Cohen, R., Gutkind, P. C. W., and Brazier, P. (eds) (1979), *Peasants and Proletarians: the Struggles of Third World Workers* (London: Hutchinson).
Cole, G. D. H., and Postgate, R. (1961), *The Common People, 1746–1946* (London: Methuen).
Connell, R. W. (1977), *Ruling Class, Ruling Culture* (Melbourne: Cambridge University Press).
Connell, R. W., and Irving, T. H. (1980), *Class Structure in Australian History: Documents, Narrative and Argument* (Melbourne: Longman Cheshire).
Cottrell, A. (1984), *Social Classes in Marxist Theory* (London: Routledge & Kegan Paul).
Cousins, J. M., and Davis, R. L. (1974), 'Working class incorporation: a historical approach', in Frank Parkin (ed.), *The Social Analysis of Class Structure* (London: Tavistock), pp. 275–97.
Dahrendorf, R. (1959), *Class and Class Conflict in an Industrial Society* (London: Routledge & Kegan Paul).
Dahrendorf, R. (1968), *Essays in the Theory of Society* (London: Routledge & Kegan Paul).
Davis, D. B. (1970), *The Problem of Slavery in Western Culture* (Harmondsworth: Penguin).
Davis, K., and Moore, W. E. (1945), 'Some principles of stratification', *American Sociological Review*, vol. 10, no. 2, pp. 242–49.
Denoon, D. (1983), *Settler Capitalism: The Dynamics of Dependent Development in the Southern Hemisphere* (Oxford: Clarendon Press).
Deshen, S., and Zenner, W. P. (eds) (1982), *Jewish Societies in the Middle East: Community, Culture and Authority* (Washington: University Press of America).
Desroche, H. (1979), *The Sociology of Hope* (London: Routledge & Kegan Paul).
Dore, R. P. (1958), *City Life in Japan* (Berkeley: University of California Press).
Dore, R. P. (ed.) (1967), *Aspects of Social Change in Modern Japan* (Princeton, NJ: Princeton University Press).
Draper, H. (1974), 'Marx on democratic forms of government', in *The Socialist Register* (London: Merlin Press), pp. 101–24.
Duncan, G. (1973), *Marx and Mill: Two Views of Social Conflict and social harmony* (London: Cambridge University Press).
Durkheim, E. (1962), *Socialism* (with an introduction by A. W. Gouldner) (New York: Collier).
Durkheim, E. (1969), 'Individualism and the intellectuals', *Political Studies*, vol. 17, pp. 14–30.
Durkheim, E. (1978), 'The conjugal family', in M. Traugott (ed.), *Emile Durkheim on Institutional Analysis* (Chicago and London: University of Chicago Press), pp. 229–39.
Dyson, K. H. F. (1980), *The State Tradition in Western Europe: A*

Study of an Idea and Institution (Oxford: Martin Robertson).
Eden, R. (1983), *Political Leadership and Nihilism: a Study of Weber and Nietzsche* (Tampa: University Presses of Florida).
Elias, N. (1983), *The Court Society* (Oxford: Blackwell).
Elkan, W. (1973), *An Introduction to Development Economics* (Harmondsworth: Penguin).
Engels, F. (1965), *The Peasant War in Germany* (Moscow: Progress Publishers).
Epstein, C. F. (1970), 'Encountering the male establishment: Sex-status limits on women's careers in the professions', *American Journal of Sociology*, vol. 75, pp. 965–82.
Eyerman, R. (1982), 'Consciousness and action: Alaine Touraine', *Thesis Eleven*, vol. 5–6, pp. 279–88.
Featherstone, M. (1983), 'Consumer culture: An introduction', *Theory, Culture and Society*, vol. 1, no. 3, pp. 4–9.
Fohlen, C. (1973), 'France 1700–1914', in C. M. Cipolla (ed.), *The Emergence of Industrial Societies* (London: Collins), pp. 7–75.
Foucault, M. (1977), *Discipline and Punish: The Birth of the Prison* (London: Tavistock).
Frank, A. G. (1967), *Capitalism and Underdevelopment in Latin America* (New York: Monthly Review Press).
Frank, A. G. (1971), *Sociology of Development and the Underdevelopment of Sociology* (London: Pluto Press).
Frank, A. G. (1982), 'After Reagonomics and Thatcherism, what?' *Thesis Eleven*, vol. 4, pp. 33–47.
French, R. D. (1975), *Antivivisection and Medical Science in Victorian Society* (Princeton, NJ: Princeton University Press).
Freund, J. (1978), 'German sociology in the time of Max Weber', in T. Bottomore and R. Nisbet (eds), *A History of Sociological Analysis* (London: Heinemann), pp. 149–86.
Fried, C. (ed.) (1982), *Minorities, Community and Identity* (Berlin: Springer).
Frisby, D. (1981), *Sociological Impressionism: A Reassessment of Georg Simmel's Social Theory* (London: Heinemann).
Gamarnikow, E. (1978), 'Sexual division of labour: the case of nursing', in Annette Kuhn and AnnMarie Wolpe (eds), *Feminism and Materialism: Women and Modes of Production* (London: Routledge & Kegan Paul), pp. 96–123.
Gamble, A., and Walton, P. (1976), *Capitalism in Crisis: Inflation and the State* (London: Macmillan).
Gay, P. (1952), *The Dilemma of Democratic Socialism: Edward Bernstein's Challenge to Marx* (New York: Columbia University Press).
Gellner, E. (1964), *Thought and Change* (London: Weidenfeld & Nicolson).
Gellner, E. (1974), *Contemporary Thought and Politics* in J. C. Jarvie and J. Agassi (eds) (London and Boston: Routledge & Kegan Paul).

Gellner, E. (1979), 'The social roots of egalitarianism', *Dialectics and Humanism*, vol. 4, pp. 27–43.
Gellner, E. (1983), *Nations and Nationalism* (Oxford: Blackwell).
Gibb, H. A. R., and Bowen, H. (1957), *Islamic Society and the West* (London: Oxford University Press).
Giddens, A. (1973), *The Class Structure of the Advanced Societies* (London: Hutchinson).
Giddens, A. (1978), *Durkheim* (London: Fontana).
Giddens, A. (1982), *Profiles and Critiques in Social Theory* (London: Macmillan).
Giddens, A. (1984), *The Constitution of Society: Outline of the Theory of Structuration* (Cambridge: Polity Press).
Giddens, A., and Held, D. (eds) (1982), *Classes, Power and Conflict: Classical and Contemporary Debates* (London: Macmillan).
Glazer, N. (1983), *Ethnic Dilemmas 1964–1982* (Cambridge, Mass.: Harvard University Press).
Glynn, A., and Sutcliffe, B. (1972), *British Capitalism, Workers and the Profit Squeeze* (Harmondsworth: Penguin).
Glynn, S., and Oxborrow, J. (1976), *Interwar Britain: A Social and Economic History* (London: Allen & Unwin).
Goldman, L. (1964), *The Hidden God* (London: Routledge & Kegan Paul).
Goldmann, L. (1973), *The Philosophy of the Enlightenment; The Christian Burgess and the Enlightenment* (London: Routledge & Kegan Paul).
Goldthorpe, J. H. (1978), 'The current inflation: towards a sociological account', in Fred Hirsch and John H. Goldthorpe (eds), *The Political Economy of Inflation* (Oxford: Martin Robertson), pp. 186–214.
Gorz, A. (1975), *Socialism and Revolution* (London: Allen Lane).
Gorz, A. (1982), *Farewell to the Working Class: An Essay on Post-Industrial Socialism* (London: Pluto Press).
Gouldner, A. (1955), 'Metaphysical pathos and the theory of bureaucracy', *American Political Science Review*, vol. 49, pp. 496–507.
Gouldner, A. W. (1967), *Enter Plato, Classical Greece and the Origins of Social Theory* (London: Routledge & Kegan Paul).
Greenberg, S. (1980), *Race and State in Capitalist Development: Comparative Perspectives* (New Haven Conn.: Yale University Press).
Gregorovius, F. (1966), *The Ghetto and the Jews of Rome* (New York: Schocken).
Grylls, D. (1978), *Guardians and Angels: Parents and Children in Nineteenth-Century Literature* (London: Faber & Faber).
Habermas, J. (1974), *Theory and Practice* (London: Heinemann Educational).
Halsey, A. H. (1978), *Change in British Society* (Oxford: Oxford University Press).
Halsey, A. H. (1984), 'T. H. Marshall: Past and present 1893–1981', *Sociology*, vol. 18, no. 1, pp. 1–18.

Halsey, A. H., and Karabel, J. (eds) (1977), *Power and Ideology in Education* (New York: Oxford University Press).

Halsey, A. H., Heath, A. F., and Ridge, J. M. (1980), *Origins and Destinations: Family, Class and Education in Modern Britain* (Oxford: Clarendon Press).

Harding, N. (1977), *Lenin's Political Thought* (London: Macmillan).

Hartz, L. (1964), *The Founding of New Societies* (New York: Harcourt, Brace & World).

Hayward, J. E. S., and Berki, R. N. (eds) (1979), *State and Society in Contemporary Europe* (Oxford: Martin Robertson).

Heath, A. (1981), *Social Mobility* (London: Fontana).

Hechter, M. (1975), *Internal Colonialism: The Celtic Fringe in British National Development 1536–1966* (London: Routledge & Kegan Paul).

Hepworth, M., and Turner, B. S. (1982), *Confession, Studies in Deviance and Religion* (London: Routledge & Kegan Paul).

Hirst, P. Q. (1982), 'The division of labour, incomes policy and industrial democracy', in Anthony Giddens and Gavin Mackenzie (eds), *Social Class and the Division of Labour* (Cambridge: Cambridge University Press), pp. 248–64.

Ho, Ping-ti (1964), *The Ladder of Success in Imperial China: Aspects of Social Mobility 1368–1911* (New York: Wiley).

Hobsbawm, E. J. (1959), *Primitive Rebels: Studies in Archaic Forms of Social Movement in the 19th and 20th Centuries* (Manchester: Manchester University Press).

Hobsbawm, E. J. (1962), *The Age of Revolution 1789–1848* (New York: Mentor).

Hobsbawm, E. J. (1964), *Labouring Men: Studies in The History of Labour* (London: Weidenfeld & Nicolson).

Hobsbawm, E. J., and Rudé, G. (1969), *Captain Swing* (London: Lawrence & Wishart).

Hofstadter, R. (1955), *Social Darwinism in American Thought* (Boston, Mass.: Beacon Press).

Hoggart, R. (1957), *The Uses of Literacy* (London: Chatto & Windus).

Hoselitz, B. F., and Moore, W. E. (eds) (1966), *Industrialization and Society* (The Hague: Monton).

Hughes, E. C., Hughes, H. M., and Deutscher, I. (1958), *Twenty Thousand Nurses Tell Their Story* (Philadelphia, Pa: Lippincott).

Hyppolite, J. (1969), *Studies on Marx and Hegel* (London: Heinemann).

Ike, N. (1973), 'War and modernization', in Robert E. Ward (ed.), *Political Development in Modern Japan* (Princeton, NJ: Princeton University Press), pp. 189–211.

Israeli, R. (1980), *Muslims in China: A Study in Cultural Confrontation* (London: Curzon Press).

Jackson, J. A. (ed.) (1969), *Migration* (Cambridge: Cambridge University Press).

Jay, M. (1973), *The Dialectical Imagination: A History of The Frankfurt School and the Institute of Social Research 1923–1950* (London: Heinemann).
Jessop, B. (1972), *Social Order, Reform and Revolution: A Power, Exchange and Institutionalisation Perspective* (London: Macmillan).
Jessop, B. (1974), *Traditionalism, Conservativism and British Political Culture* (London: Allen & Unwin).
Jessop, B. (1978), 'Capitalism and democracy: The best possible political shell?', in G. Littlejohn, B. Smart and N. Yural-Davis (eds), *Power and The State* (London: Croom Helm), pp. 10–51.
Jessop, B. (1982), *The Capitalist State, Marxist Theories and Methods* (Oxford: Martin Robertson).
Keane, J. (1984), 'Civil society and the peace movement in Britain', *Thesis Eleven*, vol. 8, pp. 5–22.
Kemeny, J. (1983), *The Great Australian Nightmare: A Critique of the Home-Ownership Ideology* (Melbourne: Georgian House).
Kettner, J. H. (1978), *The Development of American Citizenship 1608–1870* (Chapel Hill, NC: University of North Carolina Press).
King, A. Y. C., and Lee, R. P. L. (eds) (1981), *Social Life and Development in Hong Kong* (Hong Kong: Chinese University Press).
Kobrin, F. E. (1966), 'The American midwife controversy: A crisis of professionalization', *Bulletin of the History of Medicine*, vol. 40, pp. 350–63.
Kolakowsi, L. (1978), *Main Currents of Marxism, Its Rise, Growth and Dissolution*, 3 vols. (Oxford: Clarendon Press).
Konrad, G., and Szelenyi, I. (1979), *The Intellectuals on the Road to Class Power* (New York and London: Harcourt, Brace & Jovanovich).
Lacey, P. R. de, and Poole, M. E. (eds) (1979), *Mosaic or Melting Pot: Cultural Evolution in Australia* (Sydney: Harcourt, Brace & Jovanovich).
Lane, D. (1971), *The End of Inequality? Stratification Under State Socialism* (Harmondsworth: Penguin).
Laski, H. J. (1962), *The Rise of European Liberalism* (London: Allen & Unwin).
Lechner, F. (1984), 'Parsons and the common culture thesis', *Theory, Culture and Society*, vol. 2, no. 2, pp. 71–84.
Lefebvre, H. (1968), *The Sociology of Marx* (London: Allen Lane).
Leiss, W. (1972), *The Domination of Nature* (New York: George Braziller).
Lenin, V. I. (1965), *Imperialism, The Highest Stage of Capitalism* (Peking: Foreign Language Press).
Lepervanche, M. de (1984), 'Immigrants and ethnic groups', in S. Encel (ed.), *Australian Society, Introductory Essays* (Melbourne: Longman Cheshire), pp. 170–228.
Lerner, D. (1958), *The Passing of Traditional Society* (New York: Free Press).

Letwin, W. (1983), *Against Equality: Readings on Economic and Social Policy* (London: Macmillan).

Leuchtenburg, W. E. (1963), *Franklin D. Roosevelt and the New Deal* (New York: Harper).

Lewenhak, S. (1980), *Women and Work* (London: Fontana).

Lichtheim, G. (1970), *A Short History of Socialism* (London: Weidenfeld & Nicolson).

Littler, C. R. (1982), *The Development of the Labour Process in Capitalist Societies* (London: Heinemann).

Lockwood, D. (1974), 'For T. H. Marshall', *Sociology*, vol. 8, no. 3, pp. 363–67.

Lovejoy, A. O. (1938), *The Great Chain of Being: A Study in the History of an Idea* (Cambridge: Cambridge University Press).

Lukács, G. (1964), *Realism in Our Time: Literature and Class Struggle* (New York and Evanston: Harper & Row).

Lukács, G. (1971), *History and Class Consciousness* (London: Merlin Press).

Lukes, S. (1967), 'Alienation and anomie', in Peter Laswell and W. G. Runciman (eds), *Philosophy, Politics and Society* (Oxford: Blackwell), pp. 134–56.

MacIntyre, A. (1967a), *A Short History of Ethics* (London: Routledge & Kegan Paul).

MacIntyre, A. (1967b), *Secularization and Moral Change* (London: Oxford University Press).

McLellan, D. (1973), *Karl Marx, His Life and Thought* (London: Macmillan).

Macpherson, C. B. (1962), *The Political Theory of Possessive Individualism, Hobbes to Locke* (Oxford: Clarendon Press).

Macpherson, C. B. (1966), *The Real World of Democracy* (Oxford: Clarendon Press).

Macpherson, C. B. (1980), *Burke* (Oxford: Oxford University Press).

Mann, M. (1973), *Consciousness and Action Among the Western Working Class* (London: Macmillan).

Maravall, J. M. (1979), 'The limits of reformism: Parliamentary socialism and the Marxist theory of the state', *British Journal of Sociology*, vol. 30, no. 3, pp. 267–90.

Markus, G. (1978), *Marxism and Anthropology* (Assen: van Gorcum).

Marrus, M. R. (1971), *The Politics of Assimilation: The French Jewish Community at the Time of the Dreyfus Affair* (Oxford: Clarendon Press).

Marshall, G. (1984), 'On the sociology of women's unemployment, its neglect and significance', *The Sociological Review*, vol. 32, no. 2, pp. 234–59.

Marshall, T. H. (1975), *Social Policy in the Twentieth Century* (London: Hutchinson).

Marshall, T. H. (1977), *Class, Citizenship and Social Development* (Chicago and London: Chicago University Press).

References

Marshall, T. H. (1981), *The Right to Welfare and Other Essays* (London: Heinemann Educational).
Martin, J. (1981), *The Ethnic Dimension* (Sydney: Allen & Unwin).
Marx, K. (1924), *Capital: A Critical Analysis of Capitalist Production*, 3 vols (London: Lawrence & Wishart).
Marx, K. (1961), *The Civil War in the US* (New York: Citadel Press).
Marx, K. (1967), *Writings of the Young Marx on Philosophy and Society* (New York: Doubleday).
Marx, K. (1973), *Surveys From Exile, Political Writings*, vol. 2 (Harmondsworth: Penguin).
Mauss, M. (1979), *Sociology and Psychology* (London: Routledge & Kegan Paul).
Mészáros, I. (1971), 'Contingent and necessary class consciousness', in I. Mészáros (ed.), *Aspects of History and Class Consciousness* (London: Merlin Book Club), pp. 85–127.
Miliband, R. (1969), *The State in Capitalist Society* (London: Weidenfeld & Nicolson).
Miliband, R. (1982), *Capitalist Democracy in Britain* (London: Oxford University Press).
Mill, J. S. (1976), in Geraint L. Williams (ed.), *John Stuart Mill on Politics and Society* (New York: International Publications Service).
Moore, Barrington, Jr (1966), *Social Origins of Dictatorship and Democracy: Lord and Peasant in the Making of the Modern World* (Harmondsworth: Penguin).
Moore, Barrington, Jr (1972), *Reflections on the Causes of Human Misery and Upon Certain Proposals to Eliminate Them* (London: Allen Lane).
Murgatroyd, L. (1982), 'Gender and Occupational Stratification', *The Sociological Review*, vol. 30, no. 4, pp. 574–602.
Nakane, C. (1973), *Japanese Society* (Harmondsworth: Penguin).
Neuwirth, G. (1969), 'A Weberian outline of a theory of community: its application to the "Dark Ghetto"', *British Journal of Sociology*, vol. 20, pp. 148–63.
Nisbet, R. A. (1967), *The Sociological Tradition* (London: Heinemann).
Nochlin, L. (1971), *Realism* (Harmondsworth: Penguin).
Oestreich, B., and Koenigsberger, H. G. (1982), *Neostoicism and the Early Modern State* (Cambridge: Cambridge University Press).
Ortner, S. B. (1974), 'Is female to male as nature is to culture?' in M. A. Rosaldo and L. Lamphere (eds), *Women, Culture and Society* (Stanford, California, pp. 67–87.
Parkin, F. (1972), *Class Inequality and Political Order* (London: Paladin).
Parkin, F. (1979), *Marxism and Class Theory: A Bourgeois Critique* (London: Tavistock).
Parsons, T. (1942), 'Democracy and social structure in pre-Nazi Germany', *Journal of Legal and Political Sociology*, vol. 1, pp. 96–114.

Parsons, T. (1951), *The Social System* (London: Routledge & Kegan Paul).
Parsons, T. (1961), 'Some considerations on the theory of social change', *Rural Sociology*, vol. 26, no. 3, pp. 219–39.
Parsons, T. (1963), 'Christianity and modern industrial society' in E. Tiryakian (ed.), *Sociological Theory, Values and Sociocultural Change* (New York: Free Press), pp. 33–70.
Parsons, T. (1966), *Societies, Evolutionary and Comparative Perspectives* (Englewood Cliffs, NJ: Prentice-Hall).
Parsons, T. (1971), *The System of Modern Societies* (Englewood Cliffs, NJ; Prentice-Hall).
Parsons, T., and Clark, K. (eds) (1966), *The Negro American* (Boston, Mass.: Houghton Mifflin).
Peel, J. D. Y. (1971), *Herbert Spencer: The Evolution of a Sociologist* (London: Heinemann).
Petersen, W. (1958), 'A general typology of migration', *American Sociological Review*, vol. 23, pp. 256–65.
Phillips, A. W. (1958), 'The relationship between unemployment and the rate of change of money wage rates in the United Kingdom 1861–1957', *Economics*, vol. 25, pp. 283–99.
Pipes, D. (1981), *Slave Soldiers and Islam: The Genesis of a Military System* (New Haven, Conn., and London: Yale University Press).
Plamenatz, J. (1973), *Democracy and Illusion: An Examination of Certain Aspects of Modern Democratic Theory* (London: Longman).
Poll, S. (1969), *The Hasidic Community of Williamsburg: A Study in the Sociology of Religion* (New York: Schocken).
Porter, J. (1965), *The Vertical Mosaic* (Toronto: University of Toronto Press).
Poulantzas, N. (1973), *Political Power and Social Classes* (London: New Left Books; Sheed & Ward).
Pranger, R. J. (1968), *The Eclipse of Citizenship, Power and Participation in Contemporary Politics* (New York: Holt, Rinehart & Winston).
Price, A. (1974), *The Great White Walls are Built* (Canberra: Australian National University Press).
Quinney, R. (1979), *Capitalist Society, Readings for a Critical Sociology* (Homewood, Ill.: Dorsey Press).
Radice, H. (1975), *International Firms and Modern Imperialism* (Harmondsworth: Penguin).
Rex, J. (1970), *Race Relations in Sociological Theory* (London: Weidenfeld & Nicolson).
Rex, J. (1981), *Social Conflict: A Conceptual and Theoretical Analysis* (London and New York: Longman).
Robertson, R. (1978), *Meaning and Change: Explanations in the Cultural Sociology of Modern Societies* (Oxford: Blackwell).
Rodinson, M. (1973), *Israel: A Colonial-settler State?* (New York: Monad Press).

Rose, D., Vogler, C., Marshall, G., and Newby, H. (1984), 'Economic restructuring: The British experience', *Annals of the American Academy of Political and Social Science*, no. 475, pp. 137–57.

Rowley, C. D. (1975), *The Destruction of Aboriginal Society* (Sydney: Penguin).

Rudé, G. (1959), *The Crowd in the French Revolution* (London: Oxford University Press).

Rudé, G. (1964), *Revolutionary Europe 1783–1815* (London: Fontana).

Runciman, W. G. (1983), 'Capitalism without classes: The case of classical Rome', *The British Journal of Sociology*, vol. 34, no. 2, pp. 157–81.

Sabine, G. H. (1963), *A History of Political Theory* (London: Harrap).

Said, E. W. (1978), *Orientalism* (London: Routledge & Kegan Paul).

Saniel, J. M. (1965), 'The mobilization of traditional values in the modernization of Japan', in R. N. Bellah (ed.), *Religion and Progress in Modern Asia* (New York: Free Press), pp. 124–49.

Sayigh, R. (1979), *Palestinians, From Peasants to Revolutionaries* (London: Zed Press).

Scott, J. (1979), *Corporations, Classes and Capitalism* (London: Hutchinson).

Sharot, S. (1976), *Judaism: A Sociology* (Newton Abbot: David & Charles).

Shorter, E. (1977). *The Making of the Modern Family* (London: Fontana/Collins).

Shorter, E. (1982), *A History of Women's Bodies* (New York: Basic Books).

Silver, C. B. (1973), 'Salon, foyer, bureau: Women and the professions in France', *American Journal of Sociology*, vol. 78, no. 4, pp. 836–51.

Simmel, G. (1968), *The Conflict in Modern Culture and Other Essays* (New York: Teachers College Press).

Simmel, G. (1978), *The Philosophy of Money* (London: Routledge & Kegan Paul).

Skocpol, T. (1979), *States and Social Revolutions: A Comparative Analysis of France, Russia, China* (Cambridge: Cambridge University Press).

Smelser, N. J. (1962), *Theory of Collective Behaviour* (London: Routledge & Kegan Paul).

Smith, A. D. (1973), 'Nationalism and religion: the role of religious reform in the genesis of Arab and Jewish nationalism', *Archives de Sciences Sociales des Religious*, vol. 35, pp. 23–43.

Smith, G. L. (1973), *Religion and Trade in the New Netherlands* (Ithaca, NY, and London: Cornell University Press).

Sorel, G. (1961), *Reflections on Violence* (New York: Collier).

Spicker, P. (1984), *Stigma and Social Welfare* (London and Canberra: Croom Helm).

Stammer, O. (ed.) (1971), *Max Weber and Sociology Today* (Oxford: Blackwell).

Ste Croix, G. E. M. de (1981), *The Class Struggle in the Ancient Greek World from the Archaic Age to the Arab Conquests* (London: Duckworth).
Strong, T. B. (1975), *Friedrich Nietzsche and the Politics of Transfiguration* (Berkeley: University of California Press).
Tatz, C. M. (1972), *Four Kinds of Dominion* (Australia: University of New England).
Therborn, G. (1980), *The Power of Ideology and the Ideology of Power* (London: Verso).
Thompson, E. P. (1963), *The Making of the English Working Class* (London: Gollancz).
Titmus, R. M. (1963), *Essays on 'the Welfare State'* (London: Unwin University Books).
Touraine, A. (1984), 'Social Movements: Special area or central problem in sociological analysis', *Thesis Eleven*, vol. 9, pp. 5–15.
Tumin, M. M. (1970), *Readings on Social Stratification* (Englewood Cliffs, NJ: Prentice-Hall).
Turner, B. S. (1971), 'Sociological founders and precursors: the theories of religion of Emile Durkheim, Fustel de Coulanges and Ibn Khaldun', *Religion: Journal of Religion and Religions*, vol. 1, pp. 32–48.
Turner, B. S. (1974a), *Weber and Islam: A Critical Study* (London and Boston, Mass., Routledge & Kegan Paul).
Turner, B. S. (1974b), 'The concept of social "stationariness": utilitarianism and Marxism', *Science and Society*, vol. 38, no. 1, pp. 3–18.
Turner, B. S. (1976), 'Origins and traditions in Islam and Christianity', *Religion: Journal of Religion and Religions*, vol. 6, no. 1, pp. 13–30.
Turner, B. S. (1977), 'Avineri's view of Marx's theory of colonialism: Israel', *Science and Society*, vol. 40, no. 4, pp. 385–409.
Turner, B. S. (1978), *Marx and the End of Orientalism* (London: Allen & Unwin).
Turner, B. S. (1981), *For Weber, Essays on the Sociology of Fate* (London: Routledge & Kegan Paul).
Turner, B. S. (1982), 'Nietzsche, Weber and the devaluation of politics: The problem of State legitimacy', *The Sociological Review*, vol. 30, no. 3, pp. 367–391.
Turner, B. S. (1983), *Religion and Social Theory: A Materialist Perspective* (London: Heinemann).
Turner, B. S. (1984a), *Capitalism and Class in The Middle East: Theories of Social Change and Economic Development* (London: Heinemann).
Turner, B. S. (1984b), *The Body and Society: Explorations in Social Theory* (Oxford: Blackwell).
Turner, R. H., and Killian, L. M. (1957), *Collective Behaviour* (Englewood Cliffs, NJ: Prentice-Hall).
Tutt, N. (1984), 'Civil liberties and youth' in Peter Wallington (ed.), *Civil Liberties 1984* (Oxford: Martin Robertson), pp. 289–308.
Urry, J. (1981), *The Anatomy of Capitalist Societies* (London: Macmillan).

Walzer, M. (1970), *Obligations: Essays on Disobedience, War and Citizenship* (Cambridge, Mass.: Harvard University Press).
Wanlass, L. C. (1953), *History of Political Thought* (New York: Appleton-Century-Crofts).
Waxman, C. I. (1977), *The Stigma of Poverty: A Critique of Poverty Theories and Policies* (New York: Pergamon Press).
Weber, M. (1958), *The City* (New York: Free Press).
Weber, M. (1965), *The Sociology of Religion* (London: Methuen).
Wertheim, W. F. (1974), *Evolution and Revolution: The Rising Waves of Emancipation.* (Harmondsworth: Penguin).
Western, J. S. (1983), *Social Inequality in Australian Society* (London: Macmillan).
Wilkinson, P. (1971), *Social Movement* (London: Pall Mall).
Wolf, E. R. (1971), *Peasant Wars of the Twentieth Century* (London: Faber & Faber).
Wolin, S. S. (1961), *Politics and Vision: Continuity and Innovation in Western Political Thought* (London: Allen & Unwin).
Woodham-Smith, C. (1950), *Florence Nightingale (1820–1910)* (London: Constable).
Worsley, P. (1972), 'Franz Fanon and the lumpenproletariat', *The Socialist Register* (London: Merlin Press), pp. 193–230.
Zubaida, S. (ed.) (1970), *Race and Racialism* (London: Tavistock).
Zureik, E. T. (1979), *The Palestinians in Israel: A Study of Internal Colonialism* (London: Routledge & Kegan Paul).

Index

Aboriginals 78, 91, 139
abortion 105
Abrahamic faiths 16, 25, 75, 81–2
absolutism 63–4
achievement 23, 57, 113, 135
Acts
   Cruelty to animals 99
   Factory 93
   Matrimonial causes 96, 130
Adorno, T. 55, 119, 138
Almond, G. 56
Althusser, L. 4, 131
Anderson, P. 67
animals 11, 85, 89, 99–101, 127, 129–30
aristocracy 28, 67, 94, 119–20, 134, 136
Aristotle 13–14
Arnold, M. 118
art 94–5
Aurelius, M. 15
Avineri, S. 72

Bauer, B. 28–9
Bell, D. 56, 58
Benjamin, W. 55
Bentham, J. 120
Berlin, I. 65
Bernstein, E. 7–8, 11, 29, 43
Blackwell, E. 96
Blanquism 31
Bodin, J. 106
body 127–8
Bottomore, T. 90
bourgeoisie 19–20, 23, 28, 46, 63, 67, 72, 118–20, 131, 135–6, 142
Brown, M. 94
bureaucracy 55, 63, 66, 107–9, 122–14, 121–3, 135, 138, 141
Burke, E. 18

Calvinism 101, 105
capitalism 2–12, 21–5, 30–44, 48, 50–3, 55–7, 59–60, 62–3, 65, 67, 86–8, 91–2, 96, 99, 101, 103, 108, 110, 112–13, 124–5, 132, 136–42
   white settler 11, 67, 73

Carlyle, T. 118
cash nexus 23, 38
Caxton, W. 17
children 11, 14, 22, 64, 83, 89, 92–3, 96–8, 104–5, 115, 130, 134
Christianity 16–17, 73–5, 79–82, 124
citizenship 5–7, 11–26, 39–42, 44–52, 56, 59, 62–74, 76–9, 81–9, 92–100, 102–12, 115, 117–18, 120–1, 123, 127–8, 130, 132–41
city(s) 16–17, 25, 77, 79, 106, 116
city-state(s) 13–15, 17, 134
class(es) 1, 5, 8, 14, 21, 24–6, 30, 33, 35, 37, 45, 59, 63–4, 66–8, 71, 73–5, 77–8, 80, 84, 86, 88–9, 91, 93–4, 101, 112, 119, 137, 140
   middle 8–9, 11, 86, 88, 91, 93, 95, 104
   ruling 4, 11, 14–15, 34, 37
   working 2, 5–9, 20, 23–5, 27, 30–8, 42–6, 51–2, 55, 58, 66, 68–9, 72, 83, 86–7, 93–5, 98, 122, 139, 142
class conflict(s) 26, 34, 59, 62, 67–9, 71, 82, 86, 103, 132, 142
collective behaviour 89
colonial societies 78, 105
colonialism 11, 46, 61, 65–6, 76, 91, 139
consciousness 31–3, 36–7, 42–3, 68–70, 73, 87–8, 90, 107, 118, 124, 127, 129, 131, 141
consumerism 42, 49, 51
consumption 9–10, 23, 48, 61, 87
Courbet, G. 94
coverture 130

Dante, K. 101
Davis, K. 112
deindustrialization 58
de Colanges, F. 100
de Tocqueville, A. 93, 109
democracy 5–8, 10–11, 13–15, 20, 24, 30–4, 39, 44, 59, 62, 64–5, 78, 83, 93, 107, 109, 111, 122, 123, 134
de-skilling 58, 68, 105

differentiation 54
Dreyfus Affair 27, 83
Durkheim, E. 1, 20–1, 27, 66

economism 50–2
education 4, 14, 25, 31, 33, 65, 69, 86, 98, 106–8, 110, 113, 115, 118, 121–2, 131, 133
egalitarianism 16, 49, 73–5, 93, 122, 136, 139
El Greco 94
elite(s) 11, 34, 93, 116, 120
embourgeoisement 68, 87
Engels, F. 29, 31–2, 38, 66, 74, 102, 139
equality 7, 10, 18–20, 22, 24–5, 27, 50, 65, 73, 75–6, 102, 107, 109, 111–17, 119–21, 118, 135, 137–8
Euro-communism 8

fascism 30, 59, 66, 70
fatalism 54, 141
feudalism 4, 50, 67, 76–7, 101, 130
Feuerbach 32, 121
Foucault, M. 119, 122, 138
Frank, A. G. 56
fraternity 19, 111
freedom(s) 6–7, 10–11, 18, 40–1, 44, 54, 60, 70, 78, 107–8, 110, 117, 120, 134–8
functionalism 1–2, 56–7, 61, 64, 112

Gellner, E. 65, 82
gender 84, 87–8, 97, 102, 130–2
gerontocracy 49, 97, 102, 136
Giddens, A. 45–6
Ginsberg, M. 46
Goffman, E. 128
Goldthorpe, J. 45
government 40, 70, 85, 108, 110, 114, 138
Gramsci, A. 2, 33
Green Peace 104

Halifax, Marquis of 135
Halsey, A. H. 45
health 4, 70, 86, 121–2
Hegel, G. W. F. 18, 55, 65, 103
Hegelianism 28–9
Heiddeger, M. 120
Hess, M. 29
Hobbes, T. 106–7, 118–19, 135

Hobhouse, L. T. 46
Hobsbawm, E. 19
Hoggart, R. 38
Horkheimer, M. 55
Hoselitz, B. 56
housing 4, 69–70
hyphenated society 24, 37, 45, 59, 104

ideology(s) 2, 4, 10, 42, 57, 59, 64, 73–5, 78, 82, 90, 105, 110, 114, 120, 130–1, 139, 142
  dominant ideology 2–3, 11, 35, 40, 44, 52
individual 1, 5, 20, 26, 54, 82–3, 111–12, 114, 117–19, 121–3, 125, 127, 129–33, 138
individualism 21, 23, 25, 71, 79, 87, 95, 108–10, 115, 117–21, 130, 132–3, 135, 141
individuality 108–10, 118–22, 125–6, 131, 133
individuation 66, 119, 121–3, 132–3, 138
industrialization 20, 53, 55, 57, 59, 63, 66, 68, 76–7, 120, 141
inequality 5, 6, 10, 24, 27, 40, 45, 65, 73, 75, 78, 107–9, 111–13, 115–16, 122, 132, 135–7
Inkeles, A. 56
Islam 16, 75, 81–3

Jessop, R. 6
Jewish question 27–9, 82, 140
Jews 19, 26, 28, 81
Judaism 16–17, 22, 26, 28–9, 75, 81–2

Kafka, F. 55
Kant, I. 18, 21, 113, 126–7
Kautsky, K. 29, 31

labour 1, 3–4, 6–7, 14, 23, 31, 36, 38, 46, 49, 57, 61, 69, 94, 98–9, 121, 125, 140
law 4, 18, 25, 66, 96, 120
Lenin, V. 31–2, 37
Lerner, D. 56
liberalism 23, 33, 59, 76, 110
liberty 18, 20, 106, 111, 114, 135
Locke, J. 19, 93, 106, 118–20, 135
Lockwood, D. 45
Lukacs, G. 55, 114
Luxemburg, R. 31, 37

Index

market(s) (place) 1, 3–8, 10, 12, 18, 21, 23–6, 31, 38–9, 41, 45–6, 65, 79, 84, 104, 108–12, 115, 118, 120, 122, 132, 135–7, 139, 141–2
Mann, T. 55
Marshall, T. H. 5–6, 24–5, 37, 44–9, 51–2, 59–60, 64, 85–6, 88, 104, 108, 115, 121, 137
Marx, K. 3–4, 7, 20, 23, 27–30, 32, 37–8, 53, 60–2, 65, 68, 98, 102–4, 114, 121, 139–41
Marxism 2–3, 7–8, 27, 29, 33, 39, 43, 57, 60, 62, 66–7, 74, 88–9, 112, 132
Michels, R. 107
migration 26, 59, 64, 67, 71–3, 76–8, 81–2, 105
Miliband, R. 36
Mill, J. S. 53, 93, 109–10, 118
Milton, J. 101
mobility 23, 61, 71–2, 84, 115–16, 136
mobilization 61, 68, 75–6, 90
modernization 40, 56, 58–9, 61–2, 64–9, 73, 76–8, 81, 84, 105, 109, 120, 136
monetarism 5, 48, 87
Montesquieu, C. L. 19
Moore, B. 19–20, 62–4
Moore, W. E. 56, 112
Musil, R. 55

Napoleon, B. 27, 104
nation(s) 106
nationalism 1, 29, 72, 135, 140
nature 85, 91–2, 99, 124, 127, 134
Nietzsche, F. 15, 55, 118, 120, 126
Nightingale, F. 97

ownership 41–2, 95, 110, 112, 115

Parsons, T. 1–2, 16, 22, 39–40, 66, 75
parties (political) 61, 112
Pascal, B. 101
patriarchy 11, 22, 49, 70, 84, 132, 136
peasant(ry) 4, 20, 43, 57, 60, 63, 65, 67–8, 72, 76, 94
person(s) 14, 18, 26, 66, 82, 92–3, 103, 105, 108, 113, 127–33, 135–6
personality (legal) 93, 96, 100, 106, 123–8, 130–1, 135, 138
Plato 13–14
pluralism 40–1, 71–2
Poulantzos, N. 35, 120, 131

Poverty 5, 11, 58
power(s) 2, 14–15, 23, 50, 80, 84, 92, 97, 102, 104, 107, 112, 119–20
Praxis 32, 114, 121
prestige 24, 65, 112, 116
property 2, 9, 14, 21, 66, 86, 92–3, 95, 97–8, 106–7, 115, 118, 120, 130, 132, 134–7, 139

rationalization 54–5, 66, 122–3, 125, 140
Reagonomics 104
reformism 6–7, 27, 35–7, 39, 42–4, 51–2, 142
resistance 131
responsibility 125, 127, 130–1
revisionism 7, 31
revolution(s) 19–20, 29, 44, 63, 72
  bourgeois 59, 77, 134
  French 1, 18–20, 67, 104, 111, 113, 135
  Industrial 1
Rex, J. 137
rights 6–7, 10–11, 20, 22, 24–9, 34–8, 40, 42, 44–9, 51–2, 65, 68, 69–72, 76, 78, 85–6, 89, 91, 93, 95–100, 103–6, 108–11, 115–19, 121–3, 129, 132–7, 139–40, 142
romanticism 42, 126
Rousseau, J. J. 19–21, 32, 93, 106–7, 118
Rude, G. 19

secularization 49, 59, 80–1, 123, 141
Seneca, L. A. 15
sexual division of labour 70, 96, 116
Shelley, P. 118
Simmel, G. 55
slaves 14, 16, 93, 134
social change 2, 20, 54–6, 58, 61–2, 64, 67–8, 71–4, 89–90, 125
Social Darwinism 54
social membership 12–13, 16, 74, 81, 85, 92, 95, 98, 105, 135
social movements 26, 52, 74, 89–92, 95, 98, 100, 103–5, 118, 124, 127, 136–7, 139, 142
social policy 46, 70, 111, 117, 121
socialism 1, 7–8, 31, 41, 55, 112–13, 116, 138, 142
sociology 1, 2, 5, 16, 20–2, 36, 54, 56, 58, 62–3, 65, 67, 71, 86, 89, 91, 98, 100, 108, 122–7, 129, 137, 141

Sorel, G. 71
Spencer, H. 54, 93, 110
state 4–5, 9, 13, 17, 19, 21–3, 25, 28–9, 34–7, 41–2, 47, 49, 52, 55, 63, 69–70, 78–80, 82, 99, 101, 103, 106–10, 112, 121–2, 125, 130–2, 142
status 22–5, 49–50, 54, 70, 76, 78, 80–1, 84, 92, 96–7, 99–100, 103, 106, 112, 130–1, 135–6, 139, 141
stoicism 15, 79
struggle(s) 11–12, 15, 19–20, 26, 42, 45, 51–3, 61, 64–7, 70–1, 74, 76, 78, 82–6, 88, 93, 95, 97, 103–5, 139–40, 142
  working class 5, 23, 25, 35, 38–9, 43

Tasmanian Wilderness Society 104
Thatcherism 104
Tonnies, F. 54
Touraine, A. 58
trade unions 2, 5, 50, 69–70, 86

underdevelopment 47, 57, 60, 65
unemployment 4–5, 10, 40, 68, 70, 105
universalism 12, 17, 22, 71, 73–5, 79–82, 103, 139, 141
urbanization 43, 49, 59, 61, 69, 76–7

wage(s) 5, 9, 50–1, 61, 87
war(s) 20, 26, 64, 67, 69–71, 74, 77
wealth 8, 38, 40, 43, 47–8, 65, 70, 84, 87, 108, 114–15, 117, 120, 134
Weber, M. 53–5, 60, 63, 66, 75, 79–81, 101, 107, 119, 122–7, 138, 140–1
welfare (system) 5, 25, 34, 47, 49, 108–9, 136, 138
worker(s) 3–4, 9, 11, 14, 31, 37–8, 71–2, 83, 104, 136
women 11, 14, 18, 22, 70–2, 75, 81, 83, 93, 95–6, 98–9, 104–5, 116–17, 130, 134, 136
Wyclif, J. 17

Zionism 19, 29